HERS

The Wise Woman's Guide to Starting a Business on $2,000 or Less

REVISED EDITION

~

Carol Milano

ALLWORTH PRESS
NEW YORK

Published by Allworth Press
An imprint of Allworth Communications
10 East 23rd Street, New York, NY 10010

Cover design by Douglas Design, New York, NY

Book design by Sharp Des!gns, Lansing, MI

ISBN: 1-880559-67-6

Library of Congress Catalog Card Number: 96-79672

With loving gratitude to my husband Len for his encouragement and enthusiasm, and with deepest appreciation to the dozens of women who so generously shared their experiences and emotions about their businesses.

Contents

CHAPTER ONE

How You Can Start
on a Shoestring

I come from a long line of women entrepreneurs. My mother, my grandmother, and my aunt were all small-business owners, so I grew up thinking women were supposed to be their own bosses.

A lot of other American women have come to share this view—we now own more than 30 percent of the nation's sole proprietorships! According to the National Foundation for Women Business Owners, between 1986 and 1997, woman-owned businesses increased at nearly twice the national average. In the past decade, the number of woman-owned firms has grown by 78 percent. I believe this trend is the result of three factors I've been watching converge:

+ *Demographics.* For all the well-educated, success-oriented baby-boomers, the professional pyramid has narrowed. It's clear now that we can't all be CEOs of giant corporations, as there are more of us than them. Those who want the excitement of running their own show—men and women alike—are looking at the self-employment option.

- *Babies.* Many women of my generation, the post–World War II era, put off childbearing while they pursued their careers with newfound freedom and opportunity. The joys and challenges of parenthood, though, make it tougher than expected for many a thirty-five- to forty-five-year-old new mother to return to that demanding (albeit lucrative) job. Starting a home-based business often seems like an ideal way to use professional skills while still maintaining a solid chunk of family time.
- *Machines.* The ubiquity of high-tech equipment made the home office a viable way of work in the eighties. Nowadays, with a computer, fax, and modem, the sole proprietor in any isolated hamlet can communicate instantly and smoothly with any (similarly equipped) client or prospect in America! Add to this in-house capability the quick delivery offered by Federal Express, Express Mail, and their competitors, and you can truly run a business anywhere.

A key question is, should you? This book will try to help you decide that important issue. I quit my last full-time job in 1977, and have been self-employed ever since. It's very clear to me that being my own boss is the only way I'm really comfortable working. I know it's not for every woman, though. In the years I've been writing for and about small businesses, I've met, interviewed, created marketing materials for, consulted with, taught, and mingled with thousands of sole proprietors. I've watched their businesses explode, succeed, stagnate, or, sometimes, fail. Many of us started out on a shoestring. You can, too. *Hers* will show you how.

What You Need to Consider First

You don't have to wait until you win the lottery to become your own boss. You really can start a serious business with only a few hundred dollars in capital—thousands and thousands of women have. And a few men, too.

But you'll have to be realistic. Armed with only $2,000, your options, to be honest, are somewhat limited. You cannot, for example, open an elegant restaurant or launch a large manufacturing operation. On the bright side, you won't have to look for substantial loans from reluctant bankers or other investors: most women have accumulated $1,000 or $2,000 in personal savings, or can comfortably borrow it from a spouse or other relative. You'll need to adhere to what I think of as the four features of a shoestring start-up:

1. *Start out with a home office, at least at the beginning.* This offers several key advantages—it keeps your overhead low, leaving the bulk of your funds available for other business expenses; it saves commuting time, so you can put more hours into launching your enterprise; it allows maximum time with your family. Some appealing tax benefits are also possible.

2. *Choose to offer a service, rather than a product.* Producing or selling a product usually requires the purchase of equipment or inventory, which would place your enterprise beyond the $2,000 mark. A service operation could be launched with as little as a telephone, file drawer, and a typewriter or no-frills personal computer.

3. *Select a business requiring no costly equipment or inventory.* A computer-assisted data- or word-processing service is a perfect example of a home-based business. I suggested the name Burke's Bytes when Kathleen Burke launched her business. She provides word processing as well as data processing to local businesses and residents in her urban community. Her main investment, a personal computer, cost her less than $2,000. When you identify a possible service you could start in a home office, check on equipment costs first. Without renting space, that will probably be the biggest item in your budget. To control your start-up costs, you may want to look into leasing or renting high-quality equipment.

4. *Make sure the business is suited to low-cost advertising.* By selecting the kind of service business that cries out to be advertised in the

Wall Street Journal to attract the right type of client, you'll run through your entire $2,000 in capital the first month. A very specialized service firm, seeking upscale clients, may need the most expensive advertising media. On a minimal budget, you simply cannot afford television commercials, billboards, or ad space in costly publications. Look for a service business you could appropriately promote locally and inexpensively, at least at first.

I can't say I was consciously aware of all these factors of small-business start-ups when I launched my current enterprise, Milano Marketing, in 1987. Yet, my company met each of the requirements I just cited:

- It was, and remains, home based. A separate room in our brownstone is exclusively dedicated to Milano Marketing. One of the things that makes it hardest for me to consider moving the office is the incredible light in our top-floor co-op. With two windows, I can watch sunsets (since, as a typical small-business owner, I'm often working late) and keep an eye on shifts in the weather.
- My company provides a service. We create marketing materials (brochures, newsletters, sales material, direct mail, fliers, etc.) for small businesses, especially in service areas. I write copy, come up with concepts, and meet with clients. Freelance assistants, working in their own home offices, help with research and some editorial work. (While Milano Marketing often produces a product, too, by overseeing a project all the way through the design, typesetting, and printing process, the equipment for most of those activities is on my suppliers' premises, not mine.)
- We have a two-line telephone, an IBM-compatible computer and printer (which would still cost under $2,000), a state-of-the-art fax/answering machine, a full Rolodex, and other office basics. Apart from the computer, my biggest investment was in corporate identity materials. Being in an image-oriented field, I felt it was important for people to have a strong impression of the company.

Our business cards and letterhead, developed by a talented designer, are on pale blue parchment.

✦ After the computer and the parchment, there wasn't much left for advertising. I had to find inexpensive ways (which you'll read about in chapters 10 and 11) to let our target markets know we existed. I took that as a direct challenge to my ingenuity. Once we'd hit upon some effective approaches, low-cost marketing became the company's specialty!

Some women who dream of being their own bosses yearn to run a million-dollar company; others simply want a diverting part-time activity that will bring in a little additional revenue. My own goal, a challenging, fulfilling full-time career that would yield a very comfortable income, was fully met. Whatever your aim, it is possible to set up a home-based business that can reach it.

In *Hers*, you'll read about over a hundred different types of potential businesses you can consider, to start you thinking along the appropriate lines. Interviews with successful women entrepreneurs will give you insights into how they really did it, what kinds of problems they faced, and how they solved them. The book also offers guidelines on how to choose a business that's right for you.

Because *Hers* is based on a popular workshop I've taught at New York University's School of Continuing Education for many years, I've had ample opportunity to hear what concerns prospective small-business owners. The second half of the book is a step-by-step approach to actually getting started. It explains how to research your field, set up an office, and surmount some of the typical difficulties a home office may present. You'll find out how to choose a name, register your business, and develop a clientele. Two chapters focus on marketing methods and promotional strategies; plus, in this newly revised edition of *Hers*, I've included a chapter concerning that burgeoning publicity venue—the Internet. The last chapter explains where you can go for free or low-cost assistance, and the Appendix provides some further sources. I've tried to incorporate at least basic information on most questions that come up in my workshop, and direct you to a good source for more details.

I hope that *Hers* leads you to a satisfying decision about whether or not entrepreneurship is right for you, and, if so, helps you to choose the business in which you'll succeed.

∼

What Kind of Business Can You Choose?

*L*egend has it that Lillian Vernon, a doyenne of direct mail, started her vast empire by working at her kitchen table in 1951. From a home office, without expensive equipment or inventory, it is possible to run literally thousands of different businesses. For this chapter, I have selected over a hundred, just to give you an idea of the range of possible fields. Most of these are run by small-business owners who have been my clients or suppliers, or who I have interviewed for articles and books.

Some of these enterprises require a particular type of experience, training, or talent; others do not. I've divided them into four categories (businesses for everyone, creative professions, sales-related fields, and services requiring specialized training) and listed the businesses alphabetically within each section to keep the chapter unbiased and orderly.

Businesses for Everyone

I am constantly encountering businesswomen who spotted a need in the marketplace and invented, or started, a service to fill it. While none of these services require extensive training or formal credentials, it helps if you've had at least a little experience in the area, even as a volunteer. For example, if you open a gardening service, you'll have more credibility if you studied at or donated your spare time to the local botanical garden.

Sometimes women realize that what they've been doing as favors for friends—like pet training or party planning—is actually a viable service to sell to others. Many businesses have been started because the proprietor couldn't find what she needed for her own family. An example is Lick Your Chops, a gourmet pet food company, which began when founder Susan Goldstein thought a more holistic diet might help her arthritic dog. By following your own unmet needs, or listening to the wishes of your friends and neighbors, you may well be able to identify a service you could start at home to solve a particular problem. Here is an assortment of examples.

Answering Service. Are you attentive to detail? If you can make sure your telephone is covered every minute from 9:00 A.M. to 5:00 P.M., you can become a message center for small businesses in your community.

Child-Care Service. Can you recruit part- or full-time child-care providers? Then you can run a placement service by referring them to parents in need. Two working mothers I've advised for several years run, respectively, a thriving baby-sitting and a busy nanny placement firm.

Cleaning Company. Do you have access to a pool of honest, able workers who are willing to clean houses or offices? If you can handle the human resource requirement, this is a very easy business to start. I've watched one of my clients expand her business for quite a few years now.

Closet Organizer. These experts come to your home, analyze your needs, then design and install the arrangement and fixtures that will give you maximum use of your closet space.

Collection Agency. Bill collecting is a necessary but not very pleasant part of operating a business. Many firms will hire an outside agency to round up their receivables. If you never take no for an answer, you can earn a fee for collecting the money owed a company.

Corporate Gift Buyer. Often, no one on staff has the time and know-how to shop for appropriate business gifts within the allocated budget. An experienced shopper, with good taste and sources, can provide a welcome service.

Custom Tailor. If you're talented at sewing, you can provide this service for as many hours a week as your schedule permits. Assisting both men and women, you can meet with them evenings, weekends, or before they head for work. I interviewed a woman who had a full-time sales job and spent forty hours a week doing alterations and custom dressmaking.

Delivery Service. In a densely populated, affluent neighborhood in my city, a new business called Room Service operates just the way the hotel amenity does. A resident who has forgotten anything from a quart of milk to an entire shopping list can simply call Room Service, say what he or she needs, and have the items delivered to his or her door in a very short time. And, of course, Room Service follows the same sort of mark-up policy as a fine hotel—so it's a profitable enterprise!

Dog Walker. Pet owners who work long hours worry about their untended animals. If you like dogs and you're home during the day, solicit owners who will pay a weekly fee to have their pets walked on a regular schedule from Monday through Friday. A dog walker in my neighborhood often takes three out at one time. As demand (and reputation) grows, hire students to help.

Doll Hospital. Can you bring old toys back to life? A Pennsylvania woman turned her hobby into a business in the late seventies. She and her staff restore and repair all sorts of dolls and toys, shipping them to customers in other states.

Employment Agency. During the eighties, a Texas teacher started her new employment agency on $2,000. Needing a niche, she built on her knowledge of the then-new computer world, and began placing word-processing temps. Less than a decade later, her business grossed $15 million a year.

Errand Service. Busy professionals will pay for almost anything that saves them time—an irreplaceable commodity. I interviewed two women who launched successful businesses that do errands for others—anything from picking up dry cleaning to making all the arrangements for a child's birthday party or paying a parking ticket.

Event Planning. My neighbor and former client plans weddings and corporate events with incredible flair and resourcefulness. She arranges anything from a bar mitzvah to a Fortune 500 company's annual party, providing the entertainment, theme, location, food, and whatever else is needed.

Gardener. I interviewed two people who started private gardening businesses with only the money for tools and modest promotion. One was entirely self-taught. Busy people with space outdoors often lack the time to take care of a garden, but want to enjoy the beauty. If you're very good with plants and love working outdoors, this is probably a growth field for you.

Geriatric Care Provider. You've heard about the aging of America's population, the "sandwich generation," the baby boom reaching middle age. The fact is, all of us will grow older. With Americans living twenty or more years beyond retirement, a growing need exists for people who can help them in every imaginable way: psychologically, physically, and logistically. When getting around is difficult, many older people or their families will be glad to hire assistance.

Gift-Basket Maker. This service is similar to a corporate gift buyer, except it is geared toward individuals. The gift-basket maker offers the ideal assortment of appropriate goodies for a lucky recipient, thoughtfully selected and tastefully arranged in a straw basket. Some of these services have a particular theme or specialty; others provide gift baskets for any occasion.

Historical Baker. A cake can be more than a cake if you find the right gimmick. A Massachusetts woman gained instant fame in 1984 by reproducing a fruitcake from Emily Dickinson's favorite recipe. Now she sells over 10,000 of them each year. (I included this business because it may give you an idea for a baking or food-related service with a special twist.)

Kiddie Chauffeur Service. Those busy two-career couples all over America have many child-related needs. A Los Angeles woman runs a chauffeur service that picks up and delivers local children to their various schools, lessons, and play dates. As local moms get to know her and appreciate the reliable service, word of mouth has increased.

Location Scout. Someone has to find those stunning homes, sites, and gardens used for films, commercials, and print advertising. Location scouts in different parts of the country are paid a fee to find the perfect country kitchen, riverside park, or classic old barn.

Manicurist. Opening a salon would cost more than my title allows, but if you go to people's homes and offices with all your equipment, they'll pay a higher fee for the convenience.

Moving Company. One of Manhattan's best-known movers began with $12 worth of business cards and door-to-door soliciting for jobs. In a decade, the moving company grew to a fleet of fourteen trucks and sixty movers.

Moving Consultant. I created a handbook for a small firm that helps individuals and businesses organize and complete a move to a new home or office. Its owner is paid to plan and oversee all the activities involved in a comfortable relocation, including such thoughtful touches as seeing that the phone is turned on by the time the new occupants arrive.

Obedience Trainer. Geena Davis won an Academy Award when she trained William Hurt's dog in The Accidental Tourist. In real life, pet owners in many communities pay people to teach their dogs to heel, stay off the furniture, and obey commands. You have to know how to do it; a few testimonials from satisfied customers will build credibility.

Personal Shopper. Sometimes busy people don't have the time to shop for their own clothes or gifts, and they'll pay someone with good taste and fine sources to choose the right merchandise. Some personal shoppers accompany a client to assure the best selections. Personal shoppers charge either by the hour or by the project.

Plant Sitter. People away on vacations or long business trips may need someone to take care of all those indoor and outdoor plants that brighten their homes. One plant sitter I interviewed had branched out to include picking up the mail as one of her expanding services to the traveling resident.

Proofreader. If you have a good eye for detail, here is a skill that is quickly acquired through one good course. These specialists, says the Editorial Freelancers Association, "read and correct typeset material for errors and inconsistencies of spelling, grammar, punctuation, style, or fact. [The work] is done in the proof stages of preparing material for publication." The first (and very successful) proofreader I interviewed had learned the skill in one afternoon from an experienced friend who shared the basics. The demand for legal proofreaders is especially strong.

Recycling. Americans want to recycle, but desire is way ahead of the systems for implementation. A small, enterprising Oregon firm picks up used paper from businesses and carts it to a facility where it can be processed. This service is provided for a reasonable fee to the entrepreneur from each business that needs its recyclable material collected.

Renovation Service. This business is similar to general contracting in that you don't necessarily have to do the physical work, but you do have to understand it and know how to recruit, hire, and supervise a reliable crew. The female partner who chose me to write her firm's direct-mail letter wanted to stress the unique value of "a woman's touch" to her prospects.

Residential Property Manager. A home office is an easy base from which to monitor all the physical and financial needs of a group of multifamily residences. Attention to detail and ability to deal with complaints are two critical skills for a property manager; a telephone and list of reliable suppliers are crucial tools. To establish credibility, it would help to have a little on-the-job experience or a few adult education courses. If you were on the management committee of your condo or co-op building, you undoubtedly learned a great deal that would help you handle the work.

Résumé Service. You need a personal computer, a word-processing program, and a good printer (or access to a service that has one). People always need résumés and often seek help composing and printing them. It's an abundant market and a business requiring little formal training. When my desktop publisher taught a seventeen-year-old high school student to work on the résumés people brought in, she quickly learned how to do a very good job.

Scholarship Finder. Two years apart, two unacquainted women offering the identical service asked me to create their marketing materials. Both wanted to interest parents of college-bound students in purchasing a computerized search for all the available grants their children could possibly get. A national data-processing company collects all the information and performs the computerized search for each applicant. Other than knowing how to put parents at ease, this is a business requiring no special skill or training on the part of the provider, which could be easily run part-time from a home office.

Second-Home Caretaking. Those who can afford a second home may not be around often enough to maintain it, especially in winter. People who live year-round in popular second-home communities can perform a valuable service by contracting with owners to check the house on a set schedule (usually weekly or semiweekly) or making sure everything is ready for the owners' arrival.

Secretarial Service. Several years ago, I wrote a simple flier for a woman starting a home-based secretarial service in Greenwich, Connecticut. She sent her mailer to names she chose from the local phone book. A few days later, she got her first client, a world-famous entertainer. She can type, do simple bookkeeping, handle correspondence, and set up files. Generally, she works on the client's premises, using their equipment.

Swimming School for Children. Only in Southern California? During the lengthy warm season, a San Fernando Valley woman uses her own pool to teach local kids to swim. Working with up to twelve children at a time, she charges $20 for a half-hour lesson. If you're patient, a good swimmer, and a pool owner, here's a natural enterprise during the appropriate seasons. (Be sure to check with your insurance company about coverage for having all these children in your pool.)

Telephone Etiquette Coach. A St. Louis consultant grosses over $1 million a year giving telephone training seminars at corporations. She teaches employees how to handle customers more courteously and effectively on the phone. Appropriate background could be experience in customer service, fund-raising, or any other activity requiring frequent telephone contact.

Tour Guide. I consulted with a home-based tour guide who was trying to provide a unique service. Fluent in Japanese, the aspiring entrepreneur hoped to offer specialized tours to Japanese visitors, showing them whatever matched their interests. I've met other successful tour guides with precise concentrations, such as historic sites, a certain type of architecture, a particular ethnic group, celebrities, or sites of infamous crimes. This is a business with almost no overhead if you offer walking tours.

Tree Finder. When wealthy people build or buy the home of their dreams, they sometimes have their hearts set on a particular type of tree to complete the scene. If it's an unusual species that isn't sold at the local nursery, a tree scout may be hired to comb the country and find that one perfect specimen. For their expertise and custom service, tree scouts are paid well. (No, I didn't make this one up!)

Tutor. At what subjects do you excel? Could you convey the information to a child or adolescent? A tutoring business is simple to start, requiring only fliers or small ads in a local paper. The hours, given the clientele, are, of course, limited to late afternoons, evenings, and weekends. Overhead is nearly nonexistent.

Word Processor. It only seems like everybody owns a computer. Many people still don't have the time or ability to type materials they need, such as business correspondence or academic papers. Prime prospects would include students and small businesses in your community. One of my clients even word processes plays for a budding dramatist!

Creative Professions

Do you have a flair for art or design? Are you great with words or ideas? A wide range of creative fields call for exactly these abilities. Over the years, you may have developed a particular design flair as a hobby. Or perhaps you studied your area of interest in high school or college, but have not pursued it professionally.

The creative fields are unique in that if you can demonstrate the talent, clients are not so concerned with how you acquired it. Many of the businesses described in this section can be launched successfully if you take a few adult education courses in your specialty. This kind of exposure will show you how your field has evolved, give you a few sample assignments you may be able to include in your portfolio, and, most importantly, provide an opportunity for you to decide if you'd really enjoy spending long hours at this kind of activity. You'll also get the instructor's appraisal of exactly what your strengths are.

Accessory Designer. One of my clients creates fancy pins and barrettes in a small apartment. They are now being sold at stores as chic as Bergdorf Goodman.

Advertising Agency. A former client and at least six other people I know through one of my professional associations have thriving, full-service ad agencies based in their homes. These people create nationally televised commercials, as well as every imaginable type of print ad or promotion.

Aquarium Designer. One of my clients combined a hobby (fancy fish) with four years of study at the School of Visual Arts (New York City) to create a home-based career in aquatic design. That means planning, building, and stocking custom fish tanks for the homes and offices of wealthy executives, celebrities, and anyone else who can afford the service.

Art Consultant. I met with two women and one man who ran this business from their homes. They visit customers in their offices and select paintings, prints, or sculpture to match the client's taste and budget.

Caricaturist. I wrote a brochure for a woman artist who earns a living by drawing caricatures at corporate events, parties, fund-raising activities, and other celebrations. She has also branched out into providing other types of entertainment.

Cartoonist. My company's most frequent freelancer is a young, talented cartoonist who works at home.

Copywriter. With a typewriter or word processor and some good ideas, you can earn a living by composing brief material for advertising and promotional purposes. (I do!) The items you could write include newsletters, pamphlets, book jackets, direct-mail pieces, and brochures. Clients tend to be businesses.

Desktop Publisher. You'd have to buy a very simple system to keep the cost under $2,000—or head for a used computer exchange to pick up last year's model. Once you learn how to operate the equipment and programs, this is an easy and interesting business to run.

Graphic Designer. Can you create ideas and layouts for posters, business cards, brochures, book jackets, letterhead, and other printed materials? If you've got the flair, a few adult education courses can give you the know-how you need to get started. One of my collaborators is entirely self-taught as a designer. All the supplies to establish a basic studio in your home can be purchased for well under $2,000. Be sure to include the costs of some courses in your budget, too.

Illustrator. Can you draw? Being an illustrator takes talent and persistence. These days, illustrators often specialize in areas such as high-tech, medical, courtroom, or editorial work. Many professional illustrators have studios in their homes.

Interior Designer. This is a classic field for women who work at home. The designers who have been my clients were thoroughly experienced and very professional. One elected to specialize in designing children's rooms; another concentrated on commercial spaces, likes stores and galleries. You don't need any equipment to get started as an interior designer, but you do need very good taste, a knowledge of sources, and terrific listening ability so you can determine what the customer wants.

Jewelry Designer. I worked with a talented designer who made fashionable metal earrings, brooches, and necklaces at home. Exhibiting at trade shows and visiting buyers, this entrepreneurial artist was able to get fine stores to carry the lines.

Marketing Communications. Here's an enterprise I know well; it's my own. Assisted by part-time and freelance help, as needed, I create brochures, newsletters, direct-mail pieces, fliers, sales literature, and any other type of promotional material a small business might need. We are paid by the client to provide or supervise copywriting, artwork, typesetting, design, and printing. All it took was a computer, a telephone, and the right suppliers to get started.

Package Designer. I interviewed a woman who has run a successful design firm in her home for many years. She explains, "We work with boxboard, plastic, flexible packaging materials, and label design, and provide design for folders, brochures, books, and corporate identity." Her clients include famous national firms whose products you see every day.

Party Invitation Designer. An ex-fashion designer turned her hobby into a business. The Miami artist creates customized wedding invitations using ribbons, lace, or embossed flowers. They sell for $2 to $100 each. The business grosses over $2 million a year.

Photographer. If you can set up a studio in a spare room, attic, basement, or garage, you can begin doing portrait photography in your home. Some freelance photographers specialize in weddings so they can work on location. Others seek corporate work, photographing executives or events, often at the business location. A professional photographer may choose to work with products and be called upon for advertising assignments. Others do editorial work, taking pictures of news events and trying to sell them to the media. Many photographers work from studios at home.

Picture Framer. Once people know about your service, they'll be glad to let you pick up the works they want framed because your low overhead will allow your prices to be very competitive with framing shops in the neighborhood. You have to be meticulous, good with your hands, and art oriented.

Public Relations. One of my favorite start-up stories is of a determined mother who launched a public relations firm in her basement, many miles from her city's business district. Soon she bartered her services for space in a well-located office and began seriously building her company. Within five years, she was grossing over $1 million annually!

Public relations requires excellent communication abilities (both written and verbal), strong social skills, and great resourcefulness. In terms of equipment, you need a typewriter, a telephone, and a few directories on day one. To succeed, you'll need original ideas and a good list of media contacts.

Scarf Painter. A successful boutique owner told me she got her start by hand-painting scarves at her dining room table. As more and more orders came in, she had less and less living space. Soon she branched out to hand-painted T-shirts and realized she needed a manufacturing facility. When she had a full-fledged factory going, she opened a retail outlet nearby. She now sells her custom creations only in her own store to a devoted urban clientele.

Songwriting Consultant. After twenty years in the music industry, a California woman set up a consulting service for songwriters. For nearly $100 a session, she advises them on how to turn a fairly good song into a hit.

Stencil Artist. A Manhattan print artist makes tracings and rubbings from artifacts (religious charms, tribal masks, gravestones, fetishes, postage stamps) and stencils them onto T-shirts, wall hangings, canvas, scarves, and other surfaces. The work also appears on record albums, performance backdrops, and walls of stores. A wall hanging starts at $200.

Stylist. Advertising photographs and many editorial shots in magazines require the services of a professional who puts the finishing touches on the scene. Stylists make everything look just right. Often self-employed and frequently working from a home base, stylists are hired by production companies, photographers, or publications.

Tableware Designer. A neighbor I've only read about in newspapers makes napkin rings and napkins that sell for $40 to $120 retail. The former illustrator has run her home-based wholesale business for over a decade and is expanding into towel racks and Christmas ornaments.

Video Editor. If you have some experience in working with video, you can launch this business for $2,000 by either leasing the equipment or buying it used. Clients can be both amateurs and professionals with video footage who need editing services for the material.

Window Treatment Designer. A subspecialty within the design world, these are craftswomen who come in and advise clients about what to do with their windows to achieve maximum beauty, light, style, or any other goal. The window treatment designer plans and executes the concept, purchasing and installing whatever is necessary to create the finished window.

Writer. Are you good with words? It's a valuable talent in today's visual world, because verbal skills are becoming rare. With just a word-processing program, you can edit term papers for students, ghostwrite articles for businesspeople, or try to create stories you can sell to newspapers and magazines. (I learned how to market my articles in a continuing education course over twenty years ago.)

Fields for Persuasive Women

In his classic textbook, *The Successful Salesman*, Herbert Greenberg pinpoints the two traits that it takes to get people to want the product or service being offered: empathy and ego drive. Empathy means the ability to put yourself in the other person's place and to understand what the prospective buyer is thinking or feeling. Ego drive refers to having the resilience to hear a hundred people say no, without taking it personally.

Despite the sexist title of Greenberg's venerable volume, his findings apply at least as well to women. Many of us are indeed persuasive, patient, and persistent (as most mothers will attest). Sales-oriented businesses can be ideal for home-based start-ups, as they often require little capital investment. Any business will benefit from having an owner with strong sales ability, but making sales the focus of your enterprise raises a special consideration: will you enjoy selling as your main activity?

Brian Azar, a home-based sales trainer with years of experience in this field, maintains, "Everybody is in sales: art directors, receptionists, teachers—anyone whose work requires communicating with other people. I define selling as the skill or ability to communicate persuasively and effectively, to at least one other person, on a regular basis. If sales is going to be the core of your career, I add to that definition the ability to make money by communicating to others."

Dr. Azar, owner of The Sales Catalyst in Rockaway, New York, believes that to be happy in sales-related work, you must have a combination of:

- interest in being among different people and interacting with them
- effective communications skills
- desire to be outside your own office (even by telephone)
- affinity for a challenge
- need for diversity
- enjoyment of the close of a sale
- strong self-motivation
- high self-esteem

"To succeed in sales, you have to like serving people and getting paid to do it. If the money doesn't matter much, then you might as well be a social worker or waitress; they serve people but do not focus on the financial gain," Dr. Azar observes. "A successful woman running her own business usually has the ability to sell well, communicate her ideas effectively, and show enthusiasm about her product or service. You have to believe in yourself and in what you're selling," he notes.

The good news, according to Azar, is "Salespeople are born, but might forget how to do it. You can be retrained and taught." He recommends three ways to improve your sales skills, often with dramatic results:

- ✦ take a sales training course (often available at adult education programs or business information centers). Azar praises the Dale Carnegie class in selling.
- ✦ buy a book respected in the sales profession, and read it thoroughly. Azar's favorite is *Think and Grow Rich* by Napoleon Hill.
- ✦ listen to a tape about selling. Hill's classic is available on cassette.

Azar teaches a basic course in selling skills at AWED (American Women's Economic Development Corporation). About twenty-five women attend each of the two-session, six-hour classes. "A few years ago, a woman in the class was trying to start a brownie business. A single head-of-household, she'd been baking brownies for her church on weekends, then began selling them to neighbors in her Bronx community. She took the course to learn how to succeed on a broader level.

"In the first session, she got confirmation for the company name she was considering, Hill Street Brownies, which I liked because it called to mind a popular television series. For nearly thirty minutes, she practiced her 'sales interview,' rehearsing exactly what she would say to a store owner in her neighborhood when she went in to sell her brownies. After role-playing all four phases of a sales visit, she'd learned her lesson well.

"When she returned for the second session, two weeks later, she'd begun selling to local gourmet shops, delicatessens, and food stores. The class gave her other good ideas, such as a toll-free number and tips on selling by direct mail. In twelve months, she went from no income to a net profit of $40,000 the first year. Now she sends me articles that were written about her in the newspaper," Azar adds with pleasure. Here are a wide variety of businesses that rely on sales skills.

Accessories Dealer. By appointment only, a former medical researcher sells one-of-a-kind belts, bags, scarves, and jewelry—right from her apartment.

Advertising Specialty Dealer. Those key chains, calendars, and pens you've accumulated from various businesses are provided by large supply firms. One of my clients started a service that tracks down the source of any item her customer wants, at the best price available.

Art Dealer. You need a large enough space in your house, but it's certainly possible to become an art dealer without opening a gallery. I've met with three different dealers who have done it. One went on to start a commercial gallery; the other two still hold regular exhibits in their homes and sell the works of artists they have chosen to represent.

Cosmetics Distributor. One of my clients started her own cosmetics firm for well under $2,000, and handles all her sales through a network of representatives. You don't have to arrange your own manufacturing, but may want to get started as a distributor for one of the established nonretail brands.

Crafts Dealer. Through her involvement with the local arts guild, a woman I interviewed had gotten involved with rug weavers throughout her state. She now represents their work as a dealer, selling to stores and consumers.

Executive Recruiter. These specialists are paid by their corporate clients to find the right professionals for a specific executive position. Recruiters find their candidates through extensive research and networking. I know two different people who run this business from their homes. One chose to specialize in minority recruiting; the other performs high-level retainer searches for very large corporations.

Illustrator's Representative. Sometimes professional illustrators discover that selling their services is so time consuming they don't have enough hours to do their assignments! A rep functions as an agent, handling the artist's business needs, marketing her work, settling the terms of an assignment, and negotiating and collecting fees. For all this work, the rep earns a percentage of the total fee on each assignment. Reps often represent more than one illustrator, which requires more time to maintain each relationship but gives the rep an important advantage in being more likely to meet any prospective client's particular need.

Importer. A student in my Start Your Own Business class followed all the lessons and began a small business selling imported toys and ornaments out of her studio apartment in her spare time. Today, her Mexican craft items are carried by major museums and fine catalogs. Her very full-time business is booming. She has reps all over the country.

Institutional Furnishings Dealer. I recently wrote sales literature for a home-based entrepreneur who plans for and arranges the purchase of affordable, appropriate furniture for large institutions (hospitals, dormitories, rehab centers). Knowing the merchandise and where to get it is the key to operating this business.

List Broker. Colleagues constantly asked a freelance photographer who kept meticulous lists of prospective buyers if they could borrow the list. Eventually, the photographer realized a list business would be more profitable than freelance creative work, and switched careers. Home based for several years in a comfortable suburb, the list company is thriving.

Literary Agent. My first agent had a lovely, skylit home office in a historic building. Her main tools are contacts in the publishing industry, to whom she sends proposals (prepared and reproduced by the authors).

When a book is sold, the agent receives a set percentage of the advance and all royalties.

Photographer's Representative. See the description under Illustrator's Representative. Both can be done from a home office, as long as it is located near enough to the business district in your area.

Sales Trainer. I've met at length with two sales trainers, both home based and quite successful, whose clients include large corporations as well as small-business owners. They both conduct seminars and work with people on a one-to-one basis. Both are aggressive self-promoters, using everything they know about selling to build their respective businesses.

Shop-at-Home Optician. My brother-in-law, an optometrist, tells of a colleague who makes appointments to show frames at home to eyeglass wearers. A trained optician, her fee is included in the markup on the price of the frame a customer selects.

Telemarketing Service. I interviewed a woman who runs a telemarketing company from her home, supervising a group of employees who deliver a script for their corporate clients. When she started out, she made all the calls herself; as the business grew, she hired and trained others. Their minimum contract with a client requires that the telemarketing firm provide at least fifty hours of services each month.

A Little More Training . . . But Worth It

With the magic of telecommuting, almost any profession can be home based nowadays. Doctors and dentists have had office suites in their homes for decades. This last group of businesses includes those that require some kind of specialized training or certification. Some professions, like bookkeeping and image consulting, require just a few courses from a reputable institution in the field. Others, like accounting or personal fitness training, call for very specific preparation in order to be allowed to practice in your state.

If you've been using your qualifications in a staff job, you may want to consider going out on your own when the time and circumstances are right. Or you may want to start taking courses that will prepare you for a home-based business in one of these fields.

Bookkeeper. You could either travel to different small businesses to work on their books or have them send their files to your office. Two former clients run complete bookkeeping services on their home computing systems. One specializes in accounts receivable; the other offers general assistance.

Business Adviser. Accounting and law firms in the Boston area send their clients who need help starting a small business to a local business adviser. She gives them practical advice and emotional support.

Business Management Service. My firm created a mailing about a needed service for tycoons who travel a lot: management in absentia. From a home office, the owner handles business affairs for wealthy individuals when they're out of town, maintaining careful communication with them, as needed. Clients give her great autonomy and decision-making responsibility.

Career Counselor. I've worked with five different women who started career counseling firms in their homes. While none had been specifically trained in counseling, each was able to identify a specialization that drew strongly on her own professional expertise and on-the-job experience.

Casting Director. These are the people who are paid a fee to select the right actor, actress, or trained animal for each major and minor role in a film. The casting director with whom I dealt was about to celebrate her tenth anniversary in the business and had always operated it from her home.

Certified Public Accountant. I often interview a very experienced C.P.A. who operates a full-time, home-based, computerized accounting practice and has many small-business clients.

Computer Consultant. If you have expertise in some facet of the computer realm, others will need your know-how. Computer consultants do everything from designing a system for a company's particular needs, to troubleshooting when problems arise, to training the staff in how to use equipment and software. You don't need to buy your own hardware, as you would be working on the client's premises.

Copyeditor. With experience in some sort of publishing, you can meet the steady demand for freelance copyediting. The Editorial Freelancers Association reports this kind of specialist "puts material into polished form for production as a brochure, pamphlet, article, chapter, book, or other end product." As some publishers prefer their copyeditors to work on a computer, it's an advantage to have one in your home office.

Corporate Trainer. Two women for whom I write promotional materials present seminars at Fortune 500 companies. One is involved in health issues, including stress and smoking; the other specializes in communications. Both began their businesses at home.

Elevator Consultant. A fascinating part of my business is that I'm always discovering new jobs people get paid to do. One of my clients was a home-based elevator consulting firm. These are experts who know a great deal about elevators and escalators and can inspect them, diagnose problems, and recommend systems, repairs, or improvements.

Fashion Consultant. The brochure she created was stunning, and I was proud to have a hand in it. This fashion consultant (with extensive retail experience) offers her taste and style to women in their own homes. For $200 an hour, she goes through their closets, item by item, showing them what they don't need, shouldn't wear, ought to combine, etc. (While it's a limited clientele, she doesn't need many customers to earn a decent income.)

General Contractor. Traditionally a man's field, this line of work is definitely open for strong-minded women who take the trouble to learn about the business. I've written promotional material for three different women-owned contracting firms. In each case, the woman had gained her knowledge of the construction field from men, then went on to apply her own instincts and ability to making the business work. (None of these women does actual hands-on construction work, but they know how to hire crews and what to watch for as they supervise a job. They're good salespeople and managers.)

Home Haircutting. Busy people love having services provided at their convenience. If you are trained as a hairstylist, offer to meet clients in the comfort and privacy of their own homes. Of course, there's an extra charge for "house calls"!

Image Consultant. I created a brochure for a home-based image consultant who offers services to both groups and individuals. She does color and style analysis, accessorizing, and teaches makeup artistry and skin care. The training to become certified as a color and image consultant costs about $1,000.

Indexer. These are people who create a system for locating information in various types of printed materials. According to the Editorial Freelancers Association, an index is "usually produced in the form of a word-based alphabetical listing of topics, names, etc." Lately, this kind of work is often done on computers and frequently from home.

Information Broker. In our high-tech world, anything anyone wants to know is available somewhere. With all this information around, some individuals and businesses save time by turning to an information broker who knows how to access the right source for whatever a client hopes to ascertain. Many information brokers were trained as librarians. A personal computer and a modem are needed to provide this service.

Market Researcher. If you've got the credentials, a market research business is easy to operate from a home office. A lot of the work is done on-site for corporate clients who are eager to know what consumers think about their ads, slogans, and goods and services. There are two types of market research: quantitative and qualitative. The former relies on carefully developed surveys with methodically analyzed results; the latter is more freewheeling, based on structured conversations with representative consumers.

Office Organizer. For a brochure, I described the service of a consultant who comes to a small business, analyzes the operation, needs, and problems, and devises a better approach to getting the work done. She recommends methods, products, and organizational approaches to unravel each knot, build efficiency, and, often, improve morale.

Personal Fitness Trainer. This is another service affluent people will pay to have performed in their homes or offices. If you have a credential in health or exercise, this is a very lucrative branch of the field. You'll design a personal fitness program with each client, then work with him or her on a set schedule to make sure it's carried out.

Psychotherapist. Many professionals trained in social work, counseling, psychology, or psychiatry start private practices, seeing patients in groups or individually. A home office is typical. In crowded urban areas, therapists may declare a specialty: I've written promotional material for two therapists who had staked out geriatric services and interfaith counseling. Others may select marriage counseling, crisis intervention, or substance abuse as their areas of expertise.

Residential Mortgage Broker. When she went out on her own after leaving her previous employer, this M.B.A. hired me to write her brochure. With a personal computer all hooked up, she was ready to get started in her home office, helping new co-op, condo, or home buyers to find the best mortgage package available to them.

Time Management Consultant. Busy professionals and executives are sometimes overwhelmed by all the demands on their time. Experts in time management run workshops and work with people individually, helping them to find more efficient, less stressful ways to handle all their responsibilities. They are hired by professional associations, companies, and individuals.

Translation Service. I've written many mailings and ads for a home-based firm run by a couple who emigrated from Ecuador. Much of their work involves teaching executives basic business language and customs of a foreign country to which they will be traveling. They also translate legal and business documents for large, prestigious firms. Fluent in several languages, the owners hire other people to do some of the translations in languages they do not speak themselves.

～

True Stories: How Ten Women Started Their Small Businesses

*S*ome women entrepreneurs begin their companies almost by chance, others after long and careful evaluation. Certain owners are eager to be their own bosses; another segment of the self-employed accepts it reluctantly, in the absence of any alternative. I've met women entrepreneurs who fall into each category, and I'd like to share ten of their stories with you.

A striking similarity among all these owners is their enthusiasm about what they do. Even when they didn't actually say, "Oh, I love my work," the feeling was conveyed by their animation and pride as they spoke. Though the histories differ, each of the women began with very little start-up capital. You may be able to borrow some of their ideas, strategies, and solutions—or find inspiration—for your own new venture.

Art Dealer

Terry Vanderbilt was determined to quit her high-pressure job in public relations. Though she had no experience in art, it had been a longtime interest, and she decided to try buying and selling artworks. "I had a strong need to give something back to this community, to improve the quality of life," Vanderbilt reflects. She purchased a few silkscreens, limited-edition lithographs, and Japanese woodblocks, then sent out two hundred fliers announcing Vanderbilt Fine Art. "After living in the same area for fifty years, I had a lot of contacts," notes the resident of a quiet Northeastern city.

How did she learn about what she was selling? "I studied a lot," Vanderbilt recalls. Soon she was giving lectures to help people understand more about buying fine art. She was also building her mailing list and sending another flier every four months for the first two years. Vanderbilt did very limited advertising—just an occasional small ad in the local newspaper. Most of the work came by referral. Her earliest clients, homeowners and doctors, would call and describe what they wanted.

In the second year, she held an open exhibition where 250 prospective buyers came to view artworks in her home gallery. Because she is a wife and mother, Vanderbilt works by appointment only, but gives clients as much time as they need. She describes the business as "very personalized and service oriented. We find, deliver, and install each artwork, then make follow-up calls. I usually make only two appointments a day. Every job is a custom job. I do a lot of research, then handle all the framing, which we design. I have to talk about the artwork to customers and reduce their intimidation. Sometimes it's like being a psychiatrist," laughs Vanderbilt, who goes to her clients' houses. She's been asked to choose artwork for entire homes, which can take up to two and a half years. While she enjoys residential accounts, finding it "very rewarding to work with individuals," she also has commercial clients, such as banks, and has worked with other galleries.

Her gallery represents twelve local artists, and deals in European art and commissioned pieces for public buildings and private collections. She is especially proud of being asked to provide twelve major pieces of art for a new wing of a local hospital. Vanderbilt's selection of "upper-end art" includes original works, etchings, silkscreens, lithographs, oil paintings, and watercolors. She now goes to Europe once a year on a scouting trip, bringing back the kind of high-quality art that's rare in her area.

In her line of work, Vanderbilt knew it was essential to have a fine letterhead and an impressive logo. She's learned the best times to advertise are at holidays, especially Mother's Day and Father's Day. As with most service businesses, Terry Vanderbilt is involved in "a lot of legwork and unpaid time." Her specialty requires carrier's insurance.

Career Adviser

When a new director reorganized her department at a university, Debra Laks, mother of a two-year-old son, found herself unexpectedly unemployed. "I negotiated a brilliant severance package, staying on the payroll for another four months by combining vacation and sick days," recalls Laks, who was then a placement office manager.

She and her husband, an executive recruiter, had done a limited amount of résumé and job search assistance from their apartment. Clients found them through fliers at local health clubs. A perpetual networker, Laks had been mentioning to business contacts that she had "a small part-time résumé service. The day I lost my job, I had a message on my answering machine from a corporate executive I'd met with months before, telling me she knew someone who needed a new résumé. By the time I called her back, I was in business," says Laks, who considered the timely message an omen. Their part-time service had always been called Career Transition Resources (CTR), so her infant business had a name from day one.

With her son in day care, Laks bought a second couch to launch her advisement business from a home office. The same corporate contact referred a second client for career counseling. "I did lots of networking that summer," Laks remembers. She sent a mailing to everyone she or her spouse had ever met "in our whole lives!" she says. "It helped a lot that we'd run CTR as a little side business for two years. Besides getting our name around a bit, we'd had time to work out some of the kinks, like knowing how much to charge. It had given us an opportunity to test the ropes."

Laks quickly discovered how working at home differs from reporting to a job every day. "I need a lot of structure, so I re-created the department I'd run for a former employer—as head of the career counseling department—to give myself a sense of order, with room to grow. I also set aside specific days for business, several hours per day, so I didn't go from seeing a client to doing the laundry. My family had to get used to hearing me answer the phone with 'Debra Laks' instead of 'Hello.' I planned a businesslike path to the client meeting area, clearing away my kid's toys each morning."

Her initial costs were for business cards, stationery, a one-page flier, malpractice insurance, and office supplies. She didn't have a separate business phone. "I gave out the cards when I was networking with therapists, business contacts, or anyone who would listen to me," Laks explains. "I began to look for speaking opportunities and went back to clients my office had helped when I was on staff. I let them know that since they'd liked the work my team did for them, they could now hire me independently."

Laks soon detected a gap in her skills: though she considered herself strong in the résumé and job search areas, she wasn't confident as a career counselor. She identified assessment as a key area she'd need to develop to make her business grow. "Learning testing raises your rate by $20 an hour and gives you a chance to work with more long-term clients," Laks realized. She hired a supervisor to teach her assessment techniques. Sure enough, she attests, "As my confidence grew, I got more long-term clients."

Her child-care arrangements shifted to in-home baby-sitting as her client stream was increasing. It became clear that another location was needed. After only five months in operation, she rented an office in a nearby commercial building. Though it cost $500 a month, CTR broke even right away. Laks recounts, "I rented the office in about two seconds because I knew what I was looking for. The furniture to equip it and my new brochure cost over $2,000."

After a year as her own boss, Laks recognized a desire to grow. "People sought me out for jobs," she recalls, "even though I wasn't ready to sustain their salaries." Now she usually has three part-time counselors handling evening appointments; she sees people during daytime hours. She'll sometimes meet a client on a weekend if he or she can't come during the day. "I've found if you announce your hours, people accommodate. My whole reason for being in business was to set my own rules. Each of my decisions is a sacrifice of income, but I didn't go into business just to make money." The firm now sees about 150 individual clients a year, for an average of eight hour-long sessions per person. Laks herself also offers workshops for associations, universities, and corporations, which puts her in front of about 500 people each year. For CTR, these workshops bring in new clients and provide valuable new referral sources.

Her husband, Bob Marx, also works at CTR part time, which Laks admits "took a lot of debate between us. Ultimately, I couldn't have had a second child without hiring other counselors." The birth of her younger son required another adjustment in her activities at CTR. Laks used to spend about two-thirds of her time networking; now, she says, "Since the baby was born, I've done no networking. I've done some direct mail, as much public speaking as possible, and some workshops. I'm laying low, getting through the first year with a second child, and trying to keep a balance. If the workload got too heavy, I'd go nuts. I'm trying to bring on a new counselor who can generate her own referrals. Basically, I'm in a holding pattern, covering our expenses and throwing off a reasonable profit for the amount of time I put in. Before the baby, my hours were 8:00 A.M. to 6:00 P.M.; now they're 10:00 A.M. to 5:00 P.M. the days I'm in the office. Right now, I feel this the most I can handle. Because I can't increase the company's income, I'm cutting back on expenses, such as publications and associations. Luckily, I've been around long enough that the flow of clients keeps coming."

Child Care

When her daughter was born, Kathleen Lewis wanted to stay home with her baby, but she also needed to earn some money. She began offering child care to neighborhood mothers and quickly recognized a need for last-minute or erratically scheduled baby-sitters. As business burgeoned, Lewis recruited other capable women to work for her.

Before she knew it, she had more work than she could handle and decided to become a licensed agency. She took some business courses and did a great deal of research into how to operate a child-care firm. Pinch Sitters was soon the first and only agency in her city to provide nothing but temporary last-minute child care.

As demand and revenues grew, Lewis rented a small office in the neighborhood during the second year. Within twenty-four months, she was regularly arranging short-term help for more than three hundred mothers within a two-mile radius. After three years, her client roster had reached one thousand. "People call us when their regular sitters can't make it, or if the kids are too ill to go to school. Some of my clients have hectic freelance careers, or work at home and get distracted by the kids," Lewis notes.

A former model, stylist, and fashion buyer, Lewis screens her fleet of Pinch Sitters carefully. Most are college educated and have an interest in children. Typical Pinch Sitters are college students in a related field (nursing, child development) or professionals who deal with children in some way (substitute teachers, children's book illustrators). Lewis explains, "I emphasize professionals because I need people who understand commitment, being on time, and organization. They have to be able to handle babies and toddlers, since this is the bulk of my clientele." Another requirement is that they live in the communities Lewis serves, so they can get to assignments very quickly. "Pinch Sitters have to work on short notice," says its president, who begins getting requests for help at 6:00 A.M.

As a working mother herself, Lewis hires only people she'd trust with her own child. She believes being a working mother helps build rapport and trust with her clients, because "I really do understand what they're going through." Fully licensed and bonded by the city in which it operates, Pinch Sitters' service aims to make life easier for local mothers.

"You can start this business for under $1,000, with an answering machine, fliers, and ads in local newspapers. Do the baby-sitting yourself at first. As demand grows, hire other sitters," advises Lewis, who manages up to fifty Pinch Sitters at a time. She launched her company by mailing fliers in September to all the local nursery schools and day-care centers. "They hung the circulars on their bulletin boards, which gave us instant credibility," Lewis recalls.

What's the hardest part of running a child-care service? At first, Lewis found it to be a difficult balancing act. "While the business was becoming established, it was unpredictable and hard to judge how much advertising I needed to do. I'm constantly juggling between clients and sitters. I'd rather turn down a new client than hire an inappropriate sitter." She tries not to turn away clients, but it does happen. "Saturday nights are difficult and usually need to be booked far in advance," she's learned.

Lewis got a wonderful boost when her company was written up in *Parents* magazine, at the suggestion of an editor who was a Pinch Sitters client. Public response was enormous, and Lewis began offering telephone consultation to women around the country who wanted information on how to start a similar business. When she couldn't handle the stream of inquiries, she prepared an informative booklet to answer all the basic questions, and it was announced on the Letters to the Editor page of *Parents*. The booklet has sold so briskly that Lewis now plans to develop an entire series of helpful publications for parents, building on the knowledge of their needs that she's gained by running Pinch Sitters.

Errand Service

When Julie Morgenstern was a graduate theater student at the University of Chicago, she was far from home and knew no one in the entire city. That first year, "without a support system, I found myself sometimes wishing I could call a nonexistent service like Rent-a-Mom." Life improved: Morgenstern got an M.F.A. and went on to direct an Emmy-winning television series.

After getting married and having a child, she explains, "I felt the tug of wanting to be with my daughter, so I shifted to freelance work, taking two-to-three week assignments very selectively, in directing, producing, or dancing. My focus changed," Morgenstern summarizes. "I felt frustrated with my theater career because the hours are so contrary to being a mother. It's a difficult field for women to choose. When I became a single mom, it was really clear I couldn't pursue theater anymore. My daughter wouldn't even be with her father at night, and I couldn't just go off and leave her with a baby-sitter every evening."

It wasn't easy finding a new occupation. After working as a waitress for nearly a decade, during college and graduate school, Morgenstern had vowed never to do it again. While she was sorting out her options, though, she took a waitress job and danced for a large corporate entertainment company on Saturday nights when her daughter was with her father. "For five months, I bided my time to figure out what I could do. I realized theater administration, the most logical choice, paid too little to support Jesse and me." Morgenstern stayed at a hamburger joint until the end of the year.

Then one day she was empathizing with a theater friend who looked malnourished. "Come over one day. I'll make a big batch of home-cooked food for you, and you can freeze it in little portions for your meals." She and her grateful pal talked about all the overworked people who would love to have someone do home-related things for them. Suddenly, Morgenstern remembered her Rent-a-Mom fantasy from graduate school days, and a business idea was born: she would create a service to do grocery shopping, take clothes to cleaners, organize closets, plan a party, look all over for something hard to find, and handle everything a busy adult might not have time for.

Excited by the Rent-a-Mom concept, Morgenstern began planning, making notes, and studying. "I knew nothing about business—I'm a theater person," she confesses. "I bought a book on business and one on improving my vocabulary, so I could sound more professional. I went to the Small Business Administration and sought education and help for starting a business." Morgenstern soon discovered she wasn't as naive as she thought. "We all live in a business world, whether we know it or not. I've been dealing with businesspeople all my life. I'm still learning, and I love that part."

She moved on to research places to market and advertise her service, which she named Taskmasters, "because it works for both men and women." Morgenstern also set up an advantageous phone number: 855-TASK. "At first I took a classified ad, for about $20, in a local paper. On my thirtieth birthday, I got my first call from that little ad. I had targeted busy two-career parents as my market. Instead of spreading my advertising money around on a lot of little ads, I spent it all on one big ad in the local monthly newspaper for parents. I knew as a mom that it's a good publication, and people keep it around all month."

Morgenstern's first project was agonizing. She had to untangle health insurance claims for a couple who had over 250 doctor's visits between them. The husband had changed jobs twice during the time in question, and his employers had switched insurance carriers. "It was a nightmare," Morgenstern admits, "but ultimately rewarding when I got it done. Being new, I didn't charge enough." She's since corrected her pricing problem.

"A tricky thing in my business is the absence of any formulas to follow. I create a customized solution to every problem." Morgenstern's most frequent assignments are putting together albums of photos; organizing closets, cabinets, papers, and filing systems; planning parties, for kids and adults. She'll find the caterer and the site, order and address invitations, or find a calligrapher to hand-letter them. From her work with the corporate entertainment firm, she'd seen everything money could buy in the way of parties, and had kept files. "I meet with a client to select a theme and menu. I'm there during the party to keep the focus on the guest of honor so the hosts can relax," Morgenstern explains.

Taskmasters' clients pay for Morgenstern's travel time and expenses. "It's cheaper for them if I get there as fast as possible, so I rely on car service and taxis." She either bills by the hour or charges a flat rate for large projects, such as party planning. At the start of each assignment, Morgenstern discusses the anticipated time involved and the likely expenses, including charges for services like postage, photocopies, and taxis. She gets a lot of repeat business. "People can call on me for whatever they need. After the first project, I already know a lot about them and they trust me. That's when I can get very creative." Morgenstern feels clients turn to her for "all the things they feel they should have done themselves."

After setting up her pricing, Morgenstern found requests weeded themselves out. She had originally expected people to call her with needs like waiting on line for a passport, but she says, "I'm more of a home management consultant than a line waiter, at $40 to $50 an hour." In fact, Morgenstern is now hired for home renovations as a storage expert, to design, plan, and locate closets and cabinets. She interviews the residents at length to find out all about their lifestyles.

To handle requests for less expensive tasks, she set up a second service called Errand Express, with a lower rate but reliable work. "This is a separate division of Taskmasters, for more mundane chores: go to the gift shop, supermarket, or dry cleaner. We offer it three days a week, in a very defined territory. I worked out a route; part-time employees run the errands and bring everything back to my office. I do all the deliveries, from 6:00 to 8:00 each evening, when clients are home from work. I assign specific helpers to each client, so they get to know the customer's preferences," Morgenstern explains.

Errand Express customers pay $15 an hour, with an additional $5 charge for the first hour. Once Morgenstern realized the average household has two to four hours' worth of errands each week, she knew she'd found a viable market. The new service has to be promoted separately, and takes more time than Morgenstern had anticipated. "I had hoped Errand Express would promote Taskmasters and provide another kind of service people wanted. But I couldn't have afforded to run this by itself." Now that she's worked out all the kinks, Errand Express is going so well that she hopes to franchise the service in the near future.

Fashion Retailer

My favorite boutique is about two miles from my home, in a quiet, pretty, residential community. I love the distinctive natural-fiber clothes and the warm, inviting atmosphere: jazz or classical music is always playing, a beautiful cat roams the premises, and the owner is friendly but never intrusive.

I was stunned to learn that the owner had started her fashion business on next to nothing; retail clothing companies are not enterprises I would recommend to a shoestring entrepreneur. But Samone Jaspers began her business while she was an artist in Mystic, Connecticut.

"I couldn't make enough money as a painter, so I thought maybe I'd paint on silk scarves and try to sell them. By taking the scarves around to galleries and shops, I did sell a few," Jaspers recounts. "An artist friend was interested in learning how to hand-paint on cloth. We tried T-shirts because they were such a small investment. Whenever we wore them, people asked where we'd gotten them. So Chris and I bought Hanes cotton T-shirts, hand-painted them, and sold them at flea markets. Chris had an apartment in Factory Square, where the annual Mystic Art Show is held. During the show, we opened her door, put out a table stacked with our T-shirts, and sold them all. A retailer from Boston asked for a dozen, so we whipped them up and sent them to her. Then

I realized if one retailer was interested, others would be." That recognition was the beginning of Jaspers's fashion business.

"We took out a $2,000 loan so we could rent a space at the National Fashion and Boutique Show (a major trade exhibition). We built our own racks and displayed both long- and short-sleeved hand-painted T-shirts." The new venture did not even have a name before the show, but since all their painting was floral batik, they selected Fiore, which means "flower" in Italian and has a mellifluous ring to it. "At that time, everyone in Northeastern cities was wearing black and we came in with all these pastel shirts and dresses. We did $50,000 in orders at the show! Suddenly we had one hundred retail accounts. It was overwhelming," Jaspers told me.

They didn't have the money to buy the cotton clothing on which to paint their flowers, so the partners asked their new customers for 50 percent of the wholesale price up front. "We told them that if they didn't give us the money, we couldn't provide the goods," Jaspers says. With the soft pastel colors in their clothes, they landed a number of accounts in the Caribbean. (A boutique owner from one of the islands told Fiore's owners, "I figured if you had the nerve to ask for the money up front, you'd have to deliver the goods!")

The partners shifted from hand-painting to silkscreening to keep up with their orders, all of which the two women managed to deliver. Jaspers's partner was a dental hygienist with a full-time job, so Samone, who was very quick, did a lot of the artwork. They discovered virtually everything by trial and error. "We needed to learn how to ship our clothes, and found United Parcel Service doesn't go to the Caribbean. We had to learn how to count all the pieces; retailers get very upset if you accidentally send twenty-three garments instead of two dozen."

Fiore operated out of Jaspers's home until the partners moved to a little studio in downtown New London. "It was very cheap—about $75 a month at first, since New London was a depressed area then. We stayed there for about three years, while we kept trying to improve the line and design more clothing. We found an underwear factory in Pennsylvania that agreed to design simple cotton dresses for us, and then we'd decorate them. As Fiore got more involved in designing, the retailers demanded a new look every season. Our mistake was falling into the trap of all that pressure. In retrospect, what I learned was that our original concept was still valid, so I'd advise other women to go find new markets when retailers get too demanding," Jaspers reflects.

The company was about to change dramatically. Both women got divorced at around the same time. Jaspers's partner soon remarried. "With a husband in the clothing manufacturing business, Chris didn't need me anymore, so we split up." Jaspers moved to a neighboring city and went into the wholesale knitwear business, retaining the Fiore name. In one year, she and a single assistant rang up $450,000 in orders. Jaspers contracted out some of the work, hiring others to cut and sew the clothes. To meet nearly a half million dollars in orders, she signed up "with a guy who promised he'd produce all the clothes in Korea. But there were problems—with quotas, language, other things. He backed out at the last minute, leaving me unable to ship. I had no choice but to write letters of apology to all the stores. Then I went into retail," Jaspers says.

Running a boutique turned out to be a far better choice for Jaspers. "The corporate image wasn't me. I'm much more relaxed now. I do it all myself: sew, dye, design. Now I can handle it all—it's within my control." She still has time for painting. Retail clothing is somewhat seasonal, busiest at Christmas, and slow during tax season (January through mid-April). Being off the main shopping strip means Fiore gets little walk-in traffic, so Jaspers is inventive about finding ways to lure customers. For example, she'll hold a special sale soon after April 15 to entice women unwinding from the stress of income tax. She offers yoga classes in the large back room of her store, and sends monthly mailings to a house list of four hundred. A recent flier, for example, announces a Mother's Day reception, with refreshments, for a local artist whose works will be on display. A sample sale of jewelry the store normally carries will take place on another weekend. The "spring fever" sale, offering 20 to 50 percent off on many items, is the weekend after April 15. And readers are invited to visit Fiore's booth at a neighborhood public school's flea market.

Looking back at her career as a wholesaler, Jaspers comments, "There's a constant need for new ideas in fashion. Production is difficult. Dye machines are not perfect, and subcontractors trying to cut corners would dye all the tops and then all the bottoms. Sets didn't match. The market was slow. Retailers weren't calling much."

Having survived a debacle that would have sent many other business owners job-hunting, Jaspers observes, "Entrepreneurs have confidence, believe they can do something, and try to solve the problem. You don't get licked because it all seems downhill. Accountants will just look at the numbers and see if they work. But you can't just worry about money—you have to pay attention to how you're progressing." Judging from the Fiore story, it may take a few different variations of your business until you find the way it will make you happiest.

Illustrators' Representative

When Vicki Morgan started her own business, she'd learned the ropes by working for an established illustrators' representative. She left her job with the blessing of her boss, who encouraged her to go out on her own. "I'd reached a ceiling at the job. I needed more income since I was getting a divorce. At twenty-eight, I already had a reputation in the field. My rent was low at the time, and I never thought I wouldn't succeed," she says.

Morgan had taken a job as assistant to a rep because she felt it was wise to start at the bottom and learn the business from an expert. "I had the chance to represent the best talent. I have to believe in what I'm selling. My boss let me work out of my apartment since he worked out of his. He paid my expenses and we met every week or two. I was expected to be out a lot. All the phone calls came to the business number. I had my own accounts and built them from my own footwork. It was great training for my own business!

"I'd thought for about a year who I'd like to represent, then made a wish list based on the art styles I felt were most salable. I spoke to all the prospects on my list, and signed each one. After five years in the business, I knew who was available." She chose three illustrators and one still-life photographer who were not represented by anyone else.

"I went with my strengths, using the techniques that sold best when I worked for a boss. But after two years of repping both illustration and photography, I found it was divisive. My time could be better spent if I centered on one or the other. I chose illustration, because I knew it better and I felt I could bring something to the work. I knew the illustration field better from having studied art myself. Distinctions among illustrators are greater than the distinctions among photographers. I felt I could tell a client, 'There's a reason you should use this illustrator and not that one,' more than I could about a photographer."

Morgan had another reason for refining her enterprise during that third year. "I had by then felt a real sense of establishing my business. It was important to keep as much control as possible. In the studio, I'd get the job in, but the client's satisfaction hinged on the photographer's interpersonal dynamic with the client, which was beyond my control. With an illustrator, the client rarely meets the artist. Illustrators are not encumbered by having clients in their studios."

She spent the first month setting up her business: getting stationery designed, meeting with artists, organizing portfolios, choosing answering and message services, and opening accounts. Morgan had $1,500 in revolving credit and in her checking account, and was owed $3,000 in commissions from her previous job. She expected to be bringing in some earnings within three months, but recalls, "I ran the business and my life for six months on less than $7,500 total."

She made lists of people to contact based on her artists' experiences and styles and on her own research. Then she made up postcards about each artist, showing his or her work. "When I went to see people, I had a large business card (with all my artists' names) and a leave-behind about each artist."

Morgan's first assignments came from her phone calls to those ad agency art buyers and magazine art directors she felt were potential clients for the kinds of artists she represented. "I made very focused calls," Morgan maintains. "I researched which artist would be appropriate for each company I went to. They realized I could make them look good. I didn't just make blanket calls.

"On Mondays, I'd make my phone calls. The Society of Photographers' and Artists' Reps (SPAR) had lists of art directors; ad agencies would give out lists of their own art directors. I read the trade papers— I still subscribe to all of them—and went to the trade shows to see who was using what. Then I'd call and say, 'I see you use illustrators. I represent John Doe.' I'd set up appointments for Tuesday through Friday, seeing six to ten people a day. If I had empty time, I'd sit in a phone booth and make calls to firms in the vicinity."

When she started Vicki Morgan Associates, she carried all the artists' portfolios all the time. Well-known directories, like the Creative Black Book, were not yet around, so art buyers expected to see reps with portfolios. "There were no portfolio drop-offs then, either. Now it's a breeze! Over the years, directories took over. They let art directors' fingers do the walking. Clients call in portfolios after checking through the directories. I'm mostly in the office now, and I rarely see people. The pressure on my time is eased when clients ask to have a portfolio sent over," notes Morgan, adding that art directors who've been around for a long time still expect her to arrive in person. "My messenger bill each month is more than my rent! Those fees can top $10,000 a year." Morgan uses messengers to pick up and deliver artists' portfolios; out-of-town clients give their Federal Express number when requesting a portfolio for review.

"If I'm out showing portfolios, I'm not in the office handling all my other responsibilities." While she doesn't carry portfolios anymore, "I still try to pick up and deliver each job," says Morgan, who now represents eleven illustrators with a "strong design sense and elegance. Their work is classic yet contemporary," Morgan believes. She chooses her artists very carefully. "That's why it's so important for me to feel I'm in control of my business. It's a partnership with the people I represent. Neither of us is working for the other." Morgan describes a rep's role as a combination of business manager, lawyer, therapist, and salesperson. She earns a 30 percent or higher commission on each job she arranges for one of her artists. The services she performs to earn that fee include negotiating rights, arranging schedules, mailing invoices, collecting fees, sending samples, getting back original artwork, presenting and maintaining each portfolio, targeting each artist's market, and researching possible assignments.

One of a rep's important duties involves promotional efforts, such as ads and mailings. Typically, a rep pays 25 percent of the costs for a mailing to prospective clients. Expenses include printing, envelopes, and postage.

She considers her selling point the fact that Vicki Morgan Associates is a source of talent. "By calling me, the client gets Vicki Morgan plus quality, control, personality, and a high level of artist's capability." And for an artist, Morgan asserts, "A rep is your business partner—someone who takes an active interest in your career."

Management Consultant

"The last couple of years have been incredibly interesting and it looks like no end is in sight," wrote my longtime business acquaintance Eileen Morgan. "My consulting business has gone very well, and last year I worked all over the country in addition to Germany, Ireland, England, and Czechoslovakia. Perhaps the stuff I'm most excited about is the work I'm doing jointly with a Russian management consultant (who doesn't speak English, by the way). I've also been doing some training with Russian managers here on managing change and work improvement strategies, and it looks like I will be going back to Russia to work with some of the ministries and manufacturing plants! It's all being worked on now, and I should have details firmed up in a few months."

The last time Eileen and I were in regular contact, she was a vice president at Chase Manhattan Bank, working on global marketing strategies, managing operations, and handling organizational change. She did some pretty exotic traveling in those days, too. In the late eighties, she and her husband moved to Chester, Vermont, and Morgan soon set up a management training and consulting firm, The Morgan Group. According to its elegant ivory and blue brochure, the company "helps define and implement specific organizational and human resource strategies to meet management and business objectives. Often this will include highly customized training programs crafted to enrich performance and satisfaction. From needs assessments to work strategies to private and group consultations, The Morgan Group provides a corporate training ground for success."

The consulting firm was home based (in a separate bedroom) at first, but now, Morgan reports, "I have an office on Main Street, right next to the country store." The image of this far-flung consulting practice operating from Main Street in Chester, a very small town near no major business center, was intriguing. How did Morgan do this? She was happy to explain.

"I started the business by calling or writing everyone I knew in the corporate world (acquaintances, friends, colleagues) and telling them I was now doing independent consulting and had left the bank. I had a portable electric typewriter and an ancient computer printer I'd purchased used. My start-up costs were $25 for business cards. To spread the word about the business, I attended meetings and workshops and did a lot of lunchtime networking with friends and calling. This was actually my biggest expense."

Since the business moved out of the house, new clients have come strictly through referral, word of mouth, and networking. The Morgan Group is its founder's sole source of income. Gross sales are around $150,000 yearly. Morgan is delighted to talk about her work and clearly excited about the company's growth. She is also very happy living in Vermont, where the family menagerie includes a horse, dog, and cat.

Market Research

When Barbara Levy moved to San Francisco, she hoped to build on her seven years of market research experience on the East Coast. She found jobs as a research manager with several corporations and advertising agencies in the Bay Area but, unfortunately, she laments, "I hated it. After five years, I quit and traveled for six months, then decided I might as well extend the break on my résumé."

Levy went to graduate school for a master's degree in clinical psychology, having realized she was better suited to a different aspect of market research: the interviews (or qualitative side of the business). To maintain visibility in the local research community, she prepared a simple brochure that advertised, "Rent a Researcher." She landed a few consulting assignments, but "mostly I was wearing jeans and studying," she recalls. "After six years in the San Francisco research community, I was not an unknown. In my staff positions, I'd been responsible for hiring market research providers. One of the suppliers I used to employ invited me to lunch and told me his business was growing. He needed a moderator to run his focus groups and talked me into trying it—even though I'd never done that part of research."

Looking back, Levy says, "I had no idea how to go out on my own without specific experience in the service I'd be selling. I couldn't have just left my last job and started out the next day with nothing. It was easier under the aegis of someone else's business. And I was really ready to try something new. Burnt out on the business world and already separated from it as a graduate student, I was risking nothing at that point.

"Because I didn't understand how you could be a consultant and make money, I'd been thinking that I'd become a therapist. The offer from this former supplier introduced me to a new possibility. The first group I ran was very technical—management information systems managers. I'd been tired of boring statistics, but the group was fun—very dynamic and interactive, the kind of activity I'd always liked. It showed me a way that I could have the lifestyle and people interaction I wanted."

Levy maintained that first affiliation for a year, then switched to another role, in the same sort of consulting capacity. "I didn't like being the low person on the totem pole," she admits. "Getting anxious, I could see it was time to go out on my own. I realized I'd have to leave the security blanket of working for someone else. I wondered how I would get my reports typed and bound and covered, and how my invoices would get done. Recognizing I could solve those problems eventually, I started Barbara Levy Qualitative Research from an office in my home."

In retrospect, says Levy, "I can see where I underbilled at first, and gave away additional services for free. As for all those little details I worried about, a secretarial service edits and types my reports to clients. They're a fabulous addition, since I have no interest in typing, preparing, or binding reports. I draft them on my computer, print them out, bring them to my service, and they're done."

Levy runs focus groups for large corporations, including Kraft Foods, Intel, Pacific Gas & Electric, Dole Foods, and Allstate, for which she completed nine huge projects in one year. She moderates groups as large as twelve and also performs individual interviews for clients, many of them high-tech firms in the Bay Area. Levy used her twelve years' experience at large advertising agencies as a selling point. "Clients often ask what kind of experience I have with their product or service; they want to know that my background is very specific to what they sell. I'll explain that their product was a client of mine at an agency I worked for, and I try to let them know how much I understand their marketing needs. That kind of involvement really builds my credibility."

Levy reports that while focus group research firms are often mom-and-pop operations, she also competes with some well-established firms. To get clients, she contacts the company's research manager and introduces herself. "Especially when I was starting out, I stressed any experience I had in that industry," recalls Levy, who did a lot of networking at the beginning. "Because so much of my business is visibility and credibility, I went to meetings of the American Marketing Association regularly. I also keep in touch with colleagues in related areas. Working alone, it's nice to have the social contact. I've occasionally gotten business through suppliers: Toshiba found me through a facility manager. A lot of high-tech companies out here don't really have a good marketing system, so they may call a meeting facility and ask for a recommendation of a moderator. I educate potential clients, but sometimes someone else gets the business. I try not to get angry at people for taking my time. Every sales call does not lead to a sale," Levy notes philosophically.

Grateful that her business has turned out to be, as she describes, "profitable, enjoyable, fun, and an opportunity to travel, I want to pay society back for how lucky I am, by giving my skill to a worthy nonprofit organization." Levy's found pro bono work rewarding on several levels. Her project for the Boys and Girls Clubs, for example, developed her ability and experience at working with adolescents, a population with which she had no background.

"It was wonderful information for the clubs, great skill building for me, and a very gratifying experience," Levy discovered. "With a nonprofit group, the littlest bit of information from you makes a difference. It's not like dealing with clients!" She lets prospective customers know about her pro bono work, since, she says, "it shows that I am a good citizen. On the self-serving side, the board members of these charities are usually corporate executives."

Levy has found the pace of her business has quickened with the arrival of her fax machine. "I couldn't be effective without a computer and a fax because I couldn't service clients the way they expect." Her technological devices also offer an emotional bonus: "You get a sense of completion: I did it, I sent it."

Nonprofit Organization

I went to high school and college with Beth Goren, a small, ethereal-looking blonde who was always absorbed in dance and movement. Her work in these fields has taken her to some fascinating places over the years.

Goren explains, "Whenever I traveled, I would donate free services in physical fitness to senior citizens in the community. For example, when I was in Tobago, West Indies, preparing a dance performance for Montreal, I found myself offering some kind of hands-on service to elders there. I continued this involvement when I returned to Tobago a year later."

After settling in Taos, New Mexico, Goren found herself wondering, "Why do I only help elders when I travel? I decided to take a leap of faith, not worry about finances, and just go ahead. I went around the community visiting and servicing various elders, and soon started Hands-On Elders with $83."

Goren prepared a mailing to inform three hundred personal friends of the work Hands-On Elders was doing. Within six weeks, some $2,400 in contributions came in. "I handwrote the first letter, and got free photocopying on the copier in a friend's office. Our initial costs were $75 for three hundred postage stamps, $3 for three hundred plain envelopes, and $5 for the photocopy paper I had to provide in order to borrow the copier. Then, when I reached out for a sponsor, the Lama Foundation sponsored me so I could receive deductible contributions until all the corporate and nonprofit paperwork was completed. They were my umbrella for about six months."

Dedicated to serving the senior residents of Taos, Taos Pueblo, and neighboring communities, Hands-On Elders provides "a variety of specialized personal services, including gentle massage therapy, companionship, special errands, day trips, household help, reading, writing, and body-mind centering (movement and imagery for well-being)," says the agency's literature.

"We have served more than fifty elders on a regular basis during our involvement with the community. We've also taught the art of basket weaving to a group of fifteen seniors at Taos Pueblo. We have found the hands-on contact to be particularly well received by individuals with injuries, painful joints or limbs, or tense muscle areas," Goren reports.

As director, she matches volunteers and seniors "for compatible personalities so each can derive true pleasure from the experience. Some volunteers make their own contacts or join when they are already visiting an elder in the spirit of friendship and service. Many elders in our community live alone and gratefully receive visits and assistance. There are also as many people who want to help and simply need to know where to go. It's our purpose to bring these two groups together so that each can benefit.

"Our long-term goal is to provide our personalized program to as many elders in the community as possible, on a donation basis, and to expand our team in order to accomplish this task. We also envision a space to serve as an office/meeting room, with an adjoining arts and crafts center where elders can display and sell their creative work."

To launch her nonprofit organization, while under Lama's umbrella, Goren initiated the proceedings to incorporate, and talked to people in the Taos community. "We held our first volunteers' meetings at the Ten Directions Bookstore; the proprietor was my first volunteer. He visited three elder men at the Plaza Retiro (a retirement community) almost daily," the founder recalls.

Goren publicized Hands-On Elders by word of mouth around Taos Pueblo and among community senior citizens and in the local newspaper, which prints announcements at no charge for nonprofit groups. "The Taos Pueblo Indians were very open and welcoming, as they have a historic tradition of what they call hand-healing," Goren found. "Now our volunteers meet in the big art studio of ninety-three-year-old Ila McAfree, who rents me my cabin in her courtyard. We recruit via announcements in the newspaper, local bulletin boards, and word of mouth."

Hands-On Elders holds an annual fund-raiser and sends out a four-page newsletter to its supporters. "We've started sending the newsletter by bulk mail, as we can now afford the annual fee and one-time bulk cost, totaling $120," Goren reports. The group has maintained itself on a budget of $2,000 to $4,000 per year. "It's a small organization—it's personal," declares its founder. "I don't want any government funding because of the paperwork it would require. Hands-On Elders is kind of grassroots, but a real underlying support to the community at the same time." The group has amassed an outstanding library of books and tapes on aging, afterlife, prosperity, death, and meditation, which is available to both volunteers and elders. Running the organization, according to its founder, entails "some 'doing,' but a lot of 'nondoing': listening and allowing others to be involved in running the group. A lot of love and caring is also involved."

On its small budget, the nonprofit agency cannot pay its director a salary. For income, Goren teaches voice and movement classes, sees some private clients, and offers occasional basketry classes, which are popular in Taos. I interviewed Goren just before she left on a far-flung field trip. "I had given up the vision for this year, when the funding suddenly came through. I'll spend two months in Bali studying Gamelan music, seeing how elders live in that culture and are included in family and community life . . . how they participate. Then I'm going to Sydney and Melbourne for a month to teach weekend workshops (on organs, glands, voice, and movement as medicine) to the dance community. I'll be back in Taos in May. Meanwhile, the Hands-On Elders volunteers will continue their work here," Goren told me confidently.

Wholesaler/Importer

Erica Gjersvik took my six-week course on how to start a small business. At the time, she was working full time for a successful small publisher whose books and calendars were often sold in direct-mail catalogs. A Mexican crafts enthusiast, Gjersvik's fantasy was to start a mail-order business selling handmade items she'd import from different areas of Mexico.

"From my experience at the publishing company, I knew how the catalog business operated and how to work with big accounts. I was familiar with the universe of catalog buyers and what they care about. I had learned buyers' terminology and expectations and how to meet them," Gjersvik points out.

To learn about the product side of her potential business, the aspiring owner left her full-time job for a part-time position at a local shop that sold Latin American craft items. Being involved in the day-to-day activity taught her a lot about consumers' interests and preferences, while allowing her time to develop the mail-order mechanisms in her studio apartment.

She ran Pangaea part time for the first two years, slowly building accounts and a reputation. Now she rents a $2,000 booth at each semiannual International Gift Fair in New York City. "Those trade shows repeatedly put me among important buyers. Continuity brings credibility. Seeing me over and over, they know I'm part of this universe, that I've survived for a number of years. It makes a strong statement," observes the Connecticut-based wholesaler. Gjersvik follows up her trade-show stints with phone calls to buyers who visit her booth. Between shows, she sends the buyers sales letters along with samples of her products.

The approach has been very effective; Pangaea's line of handmade Mexican crafts, Christmas ornaments, and decorative accessories and gifts are featured in the nationally circulated Hammacher Schlemmer, Paragon, and Trifles catalogs, and in upscale stores like Nordstrom. "You have to know where you want to put your product, and then it helps to be in the right place at the right time," reflects Gjersvik. "In my third year, I got a number of big accounts. They'd been seeing me at trade shows, and finally responded to my follow-up efforts. The president of Hammacher Schlemmer even wanted to put one of our products on the cover of its catalog!

"I was able to build the buyers' confidence in me at the beginning by telling them who I had worked with in my job at the publishing company. I was careful never to make promises I couldn't keep, about quantity, delivery, or any other factor. I knew how often they'd been burned by false claims."

Sales representatives now call on prospects around the country. In fact, it was a rep who approached the Nordstrom buyer. "When my business was very small, I waited for reps to come to me, and took on representation groups as I could handle them. In Boston, I went to the Mart Building to find the group that had the product mix I felt mine belonged in. I hired reps in New England and Atlanta by attending trade shows in those regions and selecting possible rep groups." She's also added booths at Atlanta's Regional Gift Show and New York City's National Stationery Show to her expanding trade show calendar.

It was her passion for Mexico and its arts and crafts that had inspired Pangaea's founder to dream of running an import business. Now Gjersvik goes on two buying expeditions to Mexico each year, seeking unusual, affordable items that will appeal to her market of catalog buyers. One of her biggest challenges is finding the individual crafts-people whose products have both the right price and sophistication. She's clearly enjoying the quest—and the opportunity to earn a living by locating and selling unique, handmade items she loves to work with.

In this chapter, you've read about ten women who have discovered that owning an enterprise is the most satisfying way to work. Entre-preneurship is a very individual, personal choice. Chapter 4 will give you additional insights into the kinds of considerations that will lead you to the best decision for you.

∼

4

Is Entrepreneurship for You?

*A*re you excited about the possibility of becoming your own boss? Then this is the time to honestly assess the likelihood of your actually enjoying being a business owner. From experience and observation over the past two decades, I've assembled the key personality traits for entrepreneurial fulfillment. After reading this chapter, please take the quiz on page 71.

Before you get to the quiz, though, I'd like you to read the very personal stories of four women who made a career shift into entrepreneurship. Even though some of their circumstances were similar, each one found that owning her own business entailed some factors she had not anticipated. I believe their experiences indicate how every one of us has a totally unique perspective. I hope their candid comments will show you the array of subtle factors that need to be considered in evaluating whether or not to start your own business.

An Unplanned Event

For Debra Laks, herself a career consultant, the switch to entrepreneurship was both unexpected and frightening. "A lot of women are just not programmed to go out on their own," she reflects. "My father and his brother had gone bankrupt when they started a business, so that was my image of being self-employed. Then, while I was still very young, my father did the 'right thing' and became a social worker.

"Until I was pushed to do it by losing a job, the thought of self-employment had never occurred to me. Career counseling helped me realize I could never fit into an organization. For many women, having a child is what really puts your whole work experience into perspective. Motherhood serves as a catalyst. If I was going to work, I wanted to be enthusiastic about it," she continues.

"It was very scary to think of just being on my own. I see a lot of people looking for a partner, to share the risk.

"But that defeats the purpose. If you really want autonomy and independence, why go work with someone else? I didn't want to compromise with anyone else over a name or procedures. I wanted full control," emphasizes Laks, who is very glad she's her own boss now.

A Change from Teaching

Some women try self-employment and discover it isn't as good a match as it's been for Laks. Janet Carey had been a high school English teacher and then guidance counselor for twenty years when she took a sabbatical and started her own business. By that time, she had been the college adviser at her high school for several years and was very knowledgeable in her specialty area.

"I had met another woman who was the college counselor at a different high school. We both felt that our work involved many administrative tasks and that we'd be a good team. We were sure there was a market, since we were both approached often by people wanting advice about their kids' college educations. We anticipated a lot of demand," Carey recalls.

She and her partner were able to arrange one-year sabbaticals, at partial salary, so their housing and food costs were covered. They rented an office near Carey's home, bought furnishings as inexpensively as possible, and hired a former student to design a logo and brochure for a very low fee. During the summer, the partners sent a mass mailing to colleges to get their latest catalogs for reference, and then wrote letters to college advisers at all the high schools in their city to announce their new company. They opened their doors that September.

Looking back, Carey reports, "We ran into two killers. One was advertising. Kids are everywhere, so it's hard to focus on how to reach them. We started advertising in local weekly newspapers, but had very little luck with any of the community publications in our target neighborhoods. We got some calls from the Yellow Pages, but mostly from people who couldn't afford to pay much. Most of our clients came from word of mouth; people we knew in the field, mostly high school and college advisers, sent us referrals."

Their other nemesis turned out to be the office they'd rented so proudly. "We realized we were located at one end of a sprawling metropolitan area. Parents would have preferred that we come to their homes, so the office was actually an unnecessary expense," Carey laments.

The new firm was quoted in some articles, and Carey appeared on a few local television shows. One day, "I realized that unless we charged much more, we'd be out of business. Two people don't have enough hours in a day to bill sufficiently. We started experimenting with related services, which proved to be more lucrative. Our best gambit was preparation classes for the Scholastic Aptitude Test (SAT), which we could offer more cheaply and in smaller groups than the better-known prep courses." Since Carey had been an English teacher and her partner a math educator, they didn't have to hire instructors at first. Soon their SAT classes, running in three locations with part-time teachers, were supporting the college counseling work.

A friend led them to a major corporation to present their college advisement as a possible employee benefit. Carey took a workshop in sales presentation skills and went to professional associations where she could network or attend relevant presentations. "Parents needed to know about financial aid, so we hired specialists to provide financial aid counseling in people's homes, sharing the fee with us," Carey remembers.

Although aspects of the business were improving, the partners were still undercharging—and showing a loss. Billing remained a mystery. "In retrospect, one of the things you must do is hire professionals to guide you. We needed a marketer and an accounts person. I could never name a price," Carey says. "I discovered I'm much better at selling something other than my services. I wasn't unsuccessful; I just wasn't enjoying it. I also found, after always being part of the nonprofit world, that we were immediately suspect as capitalists. One time, we wanted to give a free seminar about college, but could never find a space we'd be allowed to use since we were not a nonprofit organization."

The partners had never prepared a budget and gradually made a significant discovery: "If we did our job right, the client would only see us one or two times. We needed constant clients," Carey realized.

At the end of their sabbatical year, it was time to make a decision about returning to their respective schools. "We could not afford not to go back to work," Carey claims. "Deep down, I don't think I'd ever seriously believed I wouldn't go back. I noticed I had consciously avoided talking with friends about how we were doing. One very successful business owner, a longtime friend, would always ask how things were going, and offer advice. I finally realized she loved this [entrepreneurial] stuff in a way that I never would."

Both women went back to the Board of Education, but they kept their office for another eighteen months, seeing clients after work. The demand was seasonal, heaviest from October to January. During that phase, Carey admits she was terrified of the business growing, requiring her to hire others while not being in total control.

On the emotional side, Carey says candidly, "Despite all the excitement of networking and business building, I found working with just one person lonely. I couldn't really socialize with the parents or kids who came to our office. I missed all the contact with my peers every day. Carol and I were a good team in that I was a people person and she's very well organized. All day, I was with either Carol or a parent who wanted something from me. I needed the constant stimulation of a busier environment. Part of what makes college counseling exciting in a school is the sheer number of people, and they all came to me. As a business owner, I felt I struggled to maintain my integrity as a counselor. Private sector clients hoped I'd take care of everything connected to the application process—including filling out the application. It is harder to educate the parent when they're paying you."

Of her year as an entrepreneur, Carey concludes, "I learned an enormous amount, and it was fun. I loved the freedom to be with grown-ups in the middle of the day at downtown restaurants. I liked not having chalk on my skirts. I enjoyed playing at business, but could see I didn't want to do it in the long haul. Despite all the frustrations of teaching, there are very few jobs where you laugh as much. Kids are funny. Things that happen in a classroom are often amusing. I missed the intrigue, politicking, and daily involvement with other people at my school. I discovered that the business world is less intimidating than I had thought, and that I needed structure. With nothing to hide behind, you really learn a lot about yourself."

She's remembered those lessons: when she took early retirement at the age of fifty-five, self-employment was not among the many options Janet Carey considered for her immediate future.

Another Ex-Educator

"I never once regretted leaving the Board of Education," exclaims Anna Elman, Janet Carey's friend and former colleague. Elman walked out on a nine-year career in education to start a business and has never looked back.

The two women met when Elman began working with foreign

students at a high school near Carey's school. Elman, who grew up in Russia, was a suburban piano teacher when she heard about the waves of Russian immigrants arriving in New York City. "I was bored with piano teaching," she remembers, "and I loved the notion of teaching newly arrived Russian kids—about the age I was when I arrived here. I was really ready to go out and work with people." Although not certified as a teacher, Elman simply showed up at South Shore High School and announced to the head of its language department all the things she could do. Impressed with her assertiveness and background, the department chairperson hired Elman to develop curriculum and teach several subjects to Russian students in a bilingual program. Soon Elman was able to get other teachers to present their own subjects to the foreign students, in English, with Elman translating.

It took five months to get on the Board of Education payroll and collect her retroactive salary, but Elman was enjoying the chance to work with receptive teenagers. She wanted to expand the program; funds were limited, so, she recalls, she started "writing proposals on my kitchen table, to get grants. We got some funds and very good press. The timing was right for Russian immigrants."

After three years at the high school, with a spectacular track record in fund-raising, Elman accepted a job as proposal writer at the central Board of Education headquarters, at double her salary. It was a good move because, Elman admits, "I was never comfortable being a teacher, but I loved working with the kids." She kept in touch with them after leaving the school.

Elman stayed at the Board of Education for six years but never took the Civil Service exams "because," she explains, "I always felt I'd leave the system one day. I got promotions and liked all my jobs, but I didn't want to feel trapped or dependent." Elman even started a unit where she had a line position, interpreting data about students and generating reports that could lead to better planning for kids from different cultures. "No one read our reports. It got very frustrating. I was with wonderful, creative people who cared about students, and sometimes in the bureaucracy, we just were not heard. I kept getting raises but couldn't stand feeling stuck. My last job at the board was assistant director in the office of University and Corporate Affairs. I had written a job description for the director position and expected to be appointed to it. We came up with great ideas, but, once again, nothing was implemented." Elman, by then divorced, began thinking about what other kind of work she could do.

For more than a year, she mulled over a possible next step. Looking back, Elman says, "It was hard to leave. The issues were meaningful, and I spent a lot of time brainstorming solutions with some terrific people—but nothing got done. I wasn't going to be fired, didn't have much money, wasn't married, and had two kids. I needed work that would provide some immediate income, but what?"

The woman who became her business partner had been saying for a long time, "We should do something together," which prodded Elman to ask herself, "What do I know how to do?" Her answers: raise money, entertain, and throw parties. A timely article in the *Wall Street Journal*, about a Chicago couple running a reunion-planning business, caught Elman's attention. "The numbers looked good, the idea made sense, and I liked the product. I knew I was good at party planning and a lot of the work could be done by computer."

Elman started her company in a spare bedroom, with "one computer someone bought me as a present, my daughter's typewriter (the only one in the house that worked), a phone, the cheapest possible answering machine, and a brochure, which found its way to the editor of the daily newspaper in my county. He liked it and passed it on to a reporter. We were interviewed in *Newsday* before we did our first reunion! The business grew from our basic idea of high school reunions. We learned by trial and error, with a lot of research and development. We didn't know much about our few competitors, and I didn't really care. In those days, there were many party planners, but few reunion companies." The original partnership dissolved very quickly, as the other woman never left her job. "She was waiting for things to happen at our company before quitting, and I kept telling her they'd happen faster if she were around full time," explains Elman, who soon found herself a sole proprietor.

Event Design Inc. grew quickly, so the owner hired helpers. The staff spilled out of the spare bedroom, then out of the newly refinished playroom, and finally took over the kitchen and other living areas. "That's when I knew we had to move out of the house," Elman observes. The company began renting office space in the next town.

Elman relishes the challenge and creativity of her business. These days, "I just consult to our reunion division. The reunions have become pretty much a package, reduced to a near science. I concentrate on special events for nonprofit organizations and corporations." Two recent projects were a big carnival for the Chemotherapy Foundation and a luau for a large advertising agency celebrating its new Dole Pineapple account—on three days' notice.

Those corporate accounts are partly a souvenir of Elman's days in education. "I had quite a few contacts from my last job at the board, where my contacts encouraged me and cheered me on. When I grew really frustrated with the board, I volunteered as managing director of an Off-Off Broadway theater company. I put its board of directors together, and it included business executives, one of whom became my first corporate client. He asked me to organize a twenty-five-year reunion of people who had worked at his advertising agency. I loved my first corporate bash, which was held in the Woolworth Mansion. I got some referrals from those theater and Board of Ed contacts; others came from word of mouth. Because Event Design tries to use very unusual spaces for parties, we get some good press based on the sites," Elman reports.

What's her favorite aspect of entrepreneurship? "The freedom of giving birth to your own ideas," Elman replies instantly. "Very little stands in the way of one of my ideas being born. I like everyone who works with me—all seven part- and full-time staff members—so it's easy to be a boss. Event Design was fun to create. I liked the name and the look, created by an artist I worked with closely. It's a very creative activity."

Elman was bubbling over about her company late one weeknight, despite having left her office after 8:00 P.M. She and a woman with whom she had worked for a long time had just formed a partnership. "She wouldn't leave until midnight sometimes. I could see she was really invested," says the founder, who likens partnership to a marriage. "I don't think you should marry someone until you've lived with him, and I don't recommend taking on a partner until you've worked together." (Elman is remarried to a man she's known for a long time.)

The company has had an annual gross of over $700,000 in recent years, and bookings look good this year. "I'm encouraged and having fun. Running a business is like being a mother: it has its ups and downs. I don't see myself as a corporate type, and I think I'm in the right business. My only fantasy of what else I could be doing is spending my time playing the piano and working in other arts areas. But a lot of that kind of creativity is used in my business, which is what makes it fun.

"Work satisfaction is my primary motive; the money is secondary. I walked out on my last job because it got hard to be there every day. Liking what you do is the most important thing," asserts Anna Elman, the proud owner of a successful business.

A Psychological Point of View

Psychotherapist Toni Heris, a specialist in career issues, is well qualified to help women weighing entrepreneurship: she's been self-employed for most of her adult life, since she was twenty-four. Dr. Heris completed a career change, at age fifty, when she earned her Ph.D. in counseling psychology after more than two decades as an advertising copywriter.

As a therapist, she finds the content of her work much more challenging. "I have always had the same excitement about learning new things," Heris observes. "If I worked for a social service agency or a hospital now, I would have certain types of clients. In private practice, I can choose my own, widely varied patients."

Reflecting on her previous career in advertising, Heris says, "Being single, I didn't have a family to feed. Risk taking has many variables. All the time I was self-employed before I got married, I was aware I had only myself to take care of. I saw single mothers who might have wanted to be self-employed but couldn't afford it. My husband, a father who had been married for a long time and was used to being the sole supporter of three people, was much less ready to be self-employed than I had been." (Heris's spouse, Dr. Stan Harrison, also returned to graduate school for a doctorate in psychology and is now in private practice.)

In her first few years after college, Heris notes, "I couldn't stand being in a large corporation. I was told to 'look the part.' I was horrified by the politics of the place. As an artistic rebel, I resented being curtailed. I found a way of surviving without all these authority figures. I like knowing I can make more money, that I'm not limited to a salary. Self-employment carries a much greater possibility of expanding your income. You have so many more options in your own business: the kinds of skills you use, the content of the work, the money you want to earn. You can make your business go in different directions as you find yourself wanting to move." After thirty years of self-employment, she has no doubt about her vocational style.

One of Heris's theories is that entry into entrepreneurship is easiest for people whose parents were their own bosses. "That family pattern sets up early expectations and role models. When I work with people who have a great deal of fear about their own business, it helps them to grasp their role models and see where the fear comes from," she explains.

Dr. Heris recalls working with a twenty-seven-year-old patient who had been an enormously successful securities trader. Married with no children, Beryl Gordon (not her real name) had lost her job. Gordon was extremely angry because, with only two years of college, she could not see any alternative job possibility.

"I gave her the Strong-Campbell Interest Inventory and her score was high in the enterprising, social, and investigative areas. She emerged as a very high entrepreneurial type with a strong scientific interest. We spent time exploring the scientific opportunities. She would, for example, have been a very likely candidate for something like veterinary training, but that was too long range. She had fairly low academic inclinations and liked immediate results, without long-range planning. Securities trading, with its fast pace, had been perfect for Gordon.

"After eliminating all the long-term possibilities, becoming her own boss emerged as a prospect. Beryl had scored high in risk taking, business management, and adventurousness. She had a lot of hesitation about this idea. Her family background was not one of risk taking. Her father worked for the post office and was very security oriented. Eventually, Gordon and her husband, a former chef and general contractor, decided to run a bed-and-breakfast establishment.

"They bought a run-down New England inn and renovated it. Both fully involved, they've created a bed and breakfast that is now prospering. The husband's family were entrepreneurs. Once we began to think of both Gordons as a team, we started to look at their combined interests. The stock market experience was important because it taught Gordon how to get loans and financial backing. Her investigative traits allowed her to search carefully for what kind of business could succeed. She read lots of magazines, newspapers, and books to glean information. Short-term research was fine for Beryl, who could explore a particular county or town for its economy and growth potential," Heris recounts.

One reason Gordon retreated from the corporate sector was her difficulty with authority figures. "She liked to do things her own way, had a hard time compromising, and had some history of conflict at work with supervisors who reduced her autonomy. I worked with Beryl every week for four months, then at six-week intervals. Her whole shift to self-employment took ten months, until she bought the inn. She had a lot of free time, being unemployed. Very focused and motivated, she wanted to make a decision and hated waiting. She dealt with it by becoming angry and active. As a therapist, I know you have to get at as much of the whole human being as you can to make sound career choices," Dr. Heris concludes.

Go over the simple quiz on the following page. Think about each item and honestly mark "Always", "Sometimes," or "Never" for each question.

Give yourself 4 points for each "Always," 2 points for "Sometimes," 0 points for "Never." If your total score is 32 or more, you probably have the key personality traits. If your score is less than 24, review the questions to make sure you were fair in your replies. If your score remains below 20, you are likely to be happier in a more secure situation.

A score of 25 to 31 suggests a closer reexamination of some of the crucial questions. I'm especially concerned about your answer to items 9 and 10. Entrepreneurs have to be optimists: if you don't believe in your product or service, how can you convince the rest of the world to buy it? Anyone who starts a business has a vision; a pessimist is unlikely to muster up the conviction to hang in until she succeeds. By definition, a new venture is a risk. If you habitually avoid risk, you may well find yourself very uncomfortable rolling the entrepreneurial dice.

In addition to risk taking, psychotherapist Toni Heris has identified five other elements vital to happiness as a business owner:

1. Comfort with a lack of structure. "You have to enjoy creating your own goals, schedule, and structure," notes Dr. Heris.
2. Willingness to be totally absorbed in your business, at least at first—"when you get very excited about what you're doing."
3. All-around problem-solving ability. "You have to be a generalist, not a specialist, because you must advertise, do budgets, and hire. Entrepreneurship taps a lot more of me than working for someone else, when my function would be more circumscribed," Heris explains.
4. Acceptance of trade-offs. "You'll have to give up some other

Is Entrepreneurship for You?

	ALWAYS	SOMETIMES	NEVER
1. Do you have a need to be in charge?	___	___	___
2. Are you a self-starter?	___	___	___
3. Were you unhappy as a subordinate?	___	___	___
4. Can you work alone, comfortably?	___	___	___
5. Are you decisive?	___	___	___
6. Do you have decent sales and negotiating skills?	___	___	___
7. Are you well organized?	___	___	___
8. Can you tolerate uncertainty or ups and downs?	___	___	___
9. Are you a risk taker?	___	___	___
10. Do people consider you an optimist?	___	___	___
SCORE	___	___	___
TOTAL SCORE	_____		

pleasures for the time being, like not going to the opera. I get so much pleasure from my practice that it's worth it. You do have to make sure to do enjoyable things on weekends. My business is very interesting to me, but a lot of people want to be finished at five o'clock."

5. Desire for variety. "In the skills you use and the work you do, it's important that you welcome diversity," Heris maintains.

So, does it seem that you have the personality to enjoy owning a business? Of course, running it successfully will take more than just the right characteristics. All the start-up steps will be detailed in chapter 7, but I'd like to comment briefly on each of the five essentials you'll need to launch your business:

- a viable idea
- ability, experience, or expertise in the area
- thorough planning, hard work, and commitment
- adequate financing to survive the first two years
- the skill to manage a new business

1. *A viable idea:* a product or service the public will buy. To determine if your idea really is viable, you need to analyze the marketplace and survey the competition. If it seems you've hit on something people will want, your first goal is to find a "Unique Selling Proposition," (a term coined at the former Ted Bates advertising agency), or a clear focus on why someone would buy this product or service from you. (See chapter 7 for more details on how to make sure your idea is feasible.)

2. *Ability, experience, or expertise in the area.* Don't open a restaurant if you've never worked in one! I always advise aspiring entrepreneurs to learn about the product or service on someone else's time. It's too expensive to teach yourself by trial and error when you're paying all the bills. Even if you've chosen a field requiring no particular training, a crucial reason to try it out before starting your own company is to

see if you like what you'd be doing all day—before you launch a business. A service that doesn't demand any particular experience (for example, plant-sitting or a message center) will certainly call for certain skills: good organizing, fine telephone techniques, or a green thumb.

3. *Thorough planning, hard work, and commitment.* Your own business, especially if it's home based, never goes away, and long hours are frequent among new entrepreneurs. Even though you won't be seeking seed money or start-up capital, I urge you to prepare a business plan just for your own use, to work out your goals, methods of operation, budget, marketing strategy, etc.

4. *Adequate financing to survive the first two years.* A standard axiom for start-ups is that the first two years' profits are plowed back into the business for more equipment, promotion, or whatever type of expansion is needed. While you may be solvent well before the two-year mark, prudence dictates that you have enough of a financial cushion to sustain you for more than the first few months. This might be your savings, a severance package from your last employer, a small inheritance, or a part-time job. Many new service firms begin with one bread-and-butter account. If you have a working spouse, his second income will really mean a lot, but I have to warn you to make sure your mate is supportive of your becoming an entrepreneur.

5. *The skill to manage a new business.* The good news about this requirement is that these are skills you can hone at workshops, adult education classes, and conferences, or with good video and cassette tapes. You'll have to either develop competency in the following areas or pay others to perform these tasks for you:

+ budgeting
+ purchasing
+ office management/administration
+ marketing
+ advertising
+ selling
+ negotiating

- communicating
- record-keeping, billing, and collecting

I can't really classify "networking" as a required day-to-day ability, but what an asset! It's a little like being naturally well organized or good on the phone—you can succeed in business without the trait, but work will be much easier if you were born being good at these skills. Chapter 10 will give you some cues about how to network effectively.

~

How to Choose Your Business

*B*efore shifting to a business that centers on my writing talents, I was a career counselor for ten years. I took vocational theory courses in graduate school, attended professional seminars, and collaborated with talented peers. In all those years, I never heard a better approach to identifying the right field than the simple method one of my colleagues at the School of Visual Arts explains to my class every semester.

Sam Viviano, a humorous illustrator whose work you've seen on many movie posters and magazine covers, tells my students that when he arrived in New York from Ann Arbor, Michigan, straight out of college, he soon realized he'd better face some facts about real life. He devised a stark, direct series of questions to help himself hone in on what became his career:

- What do I like to do?
- What do I do well?
- What will people pay me to do?

Viviano was fortunate because the same answer emerged for all three queries: caricatures. Reasoning that fees would be higher and work more constant from commercial rather than individual clients, his next task was identifying the kinds of businesses that could use this service, and figuring out ways to let them know his talent was available to them.

Every entrepreneur who ever turned a hobby into a business, consciously or unconsciously, went through a similar sequence of soul-searching, to reach the conclusion that what he or she loved to do was something a segment of the public would buy. For most of us, though, the process is not as easy as it was for Viviano and former hobbyists. In my own case, when I recognized it was time to leave career counseling, I not only knew just which questions to ask myself, but also how blind we mortals can be to our own follies and virtues.

A Choice Requiring Modifications

What I like to do, I dutifully jotted down, is solve people's problems and write. What do I do well? Write and solve problems—especially related to work. What will people pay me to do? Find creative solutions to business problems, with my writing skills as a tool? That's not exactly a field, so I asked some career counselor colleagues for input. Several of them told me I had an asset I had totally ignored: networking. Adding the facility to make contacts to the talents I'd already identified pointed plainly to one specific field: public relations.

I actually had a little experience in public relations, having served as publicist to a then-struggling film company for a year in the early seventies. I'd also written brochures and promotional materials for a few of my counseling clients who owned small businesses. It seemed like a field I could enter easily; I had all the right skills and personality traits.

With great enthusiasm, I launched my new enterprise, began soliciting clients, and did fairly well for a beginner. Despite the promising situation, I was very unhappy. I finally figured out what was wrong: though I had a perfect profile for public relations, I hadn't bothered to test this theory by following my own advice and taking the time to work for someone else to see if the industry and I were indeed a match.

On my own time, I discovered we were not. A requirement in public relations is patient cultivation of media decision makers who can choose to accept the ideas you propose. I enjoy short, finite projects, where I have most of the responsibility for the end result. Though I was good at chatting with editors, I felt I had no control over their decisions, and it drove me crazy. I rarely got any satisfaction from my efforts, and it was soon obvious I'd somehow made the wrong choice for my second business.

Reevaluating the Business Idea

With the added fact that I need to be in control of the finished product, I went back to my original replies to those three questions. What else would people pay me to do that required both writing and problem-solving skills? I allowed that perhaps my networking flair need not be a part of the service I would sell, but merely a helpful tool in marketing my business.

As soon as I thought of marketing, I sensed I'd hit on the right combination. As a career counselor, I'd spent ten years teaching professionals to set goals and market themselves to employers. Specializing in self-employed professionals, I had done extensive research to develop workshops that would help them build their businesses. I'd solved many of their internal and external problems as budding entrepreneurs. By shifting my own consulting practice away from the counseling aspect and more toward written material, I could focus on creating marketing plans, sales literature, brochures, and whatever else a small business needed to grow.

This felt like—and indeed turned out to be—a 100 percent accurate assessment of where my talents and yearnings meet the marketplace. I only wish I'd synthesized a way to write and help businesspeople years earlier, but I'm glad I finally found the profession that's perfect for me.

I did have to make one more refinement during the second year of what is now called Milano Marketing. Because of all my experience with and affinity for creative professionals, I elected to target them as my client base. Eventually, that became a market segment that was both too small and too undercapitalized. I expanded my prospect pool when I opted to make small businesses my target customers. America has many millions of small businesses, with new ones opening every day, no matter what state the economy is in.

Determining Your Own Possibilities

To zero in on a kind of business with potential for you, start out with the three questions Sam Viviano poses. Write as many answers as you can for each. Think of all the skills you enjoy using, no matter how unbusinesslike they may seem. Then write down everything you've ever been told you're good at, and ask friends for additional suggestions; because we take for granted the things we do most easily, you're likely to forget those talents. The most objective list will be the one involving what people might actually pay you to do, since that's where external reality enters the picture.

This is not a test; there are no right or wrong answers. When you have more than three answers in each column, take all your replies and look for related fields that appear on more than one of your lists. Browse through the sample businesses in chapter 2 for some ideas of enterprises that sound related to your interests or abilities. You may want to visit a career library, which will have reference materials that arrange different lines of work by the skills or interests they involve.

On the next page is a set of responses from someone trying to identify an enterprise using some of the businesses suggested by her lists. On the last page of this chapter is a blank self-profile for you to fill in.

Her next step involved going to a career library and looking up additional information about these fields or specialties. While all of these might be satisfying careers for her, some turned out to be too expensive to start as a business. She rejected those that require lengthy professional training, such as physical therapy and dance therapy, and

Self-Profile

What Do I Like to Do?

Interact with other people

Take part in sports

Keep up with current events

Read mystery novels

Dance

Sail

Solve people's problems

What Do I Do Well?

Work with people

Listen to others

Analyze sports with a technician's eye

Solve personal problems

Cook

Calm people when they are upset

What Will People Pay Me to Do?

Counsel

Run a sports clinic for senior citizens

Be a psychotherapist for athletes

Become a personal fitness trainer

Physical therapy

Dance therapy

Teach sailing (run a sailing school)

Coach a sport

found that a sailing school would demand prohibitively expensive insurance coverage. Starting a sports clinic for active adults over the age of sixty-five and helping them adapt their activities to their physical abilities emerged as a very likely enterprise. After thoughtful evaluation of the requirements, she arrived at an innovative, affordable way to test the viability of this idea in her target community: she would arrange to start it on a part-time basis at an established sporting goods store or a senior citizens' center.

How to Broaden Your Range of Choices

If you think you'd like to start a business, but answering the three questions does not suggest a particular field, I have a sincere recommendation. Sign up for either group or individual career counseling at the nearest reputable place that provides it. I worked in this field for a decade and I know how valuable competent career guidance can be. In a few individual sessions, you will have the undivided attention of someone trained to assess your needs and interests in the context of the current marketplace. In a workshop, you can get the benefit of ten or fifteen other people's experiences as they tell you what kinds of activities they have seen that would require your experience or ability. Check the Yellow Pages under "Career and Vocational Guidance" for sources in your area, and ask friends or neighbors for specific recommendations. Chapter 7 will describe all the ways to research the field you're planning to enter, but first let's look at the impact your new business can have on your personal life.

∾

Your Self-Profile

What Do I Like to Do?

What Do I Do Well?

What Will People Pay Me to Do?

Changes in Your Lifestyle

*E*arly in my workshops on starting your own business, I ask participants to list the benefits of becoming an entrepreneur. As we discuss them, the most prevalent myths about self-employment invariably emerge. Here they are:

Myth #1. You're the boss. While this is undeniable, and a very pleasant feeling at times, as a sole proprietor with a staff of one, the appropriate question may be, "The boss of what?" Once I learned that I wore all the hats around my office, I had to admit that I was the president, secretary, and janitor—and I was not equally fond of all the roles.

Myth #2. You get rich. This is a popular American fantasy, and indeed we've all heard of the pioneers who actually made their tiny ventures turn into fortunes: Mary Kay Ash, Lillian Vernon, Steven Jobs, among many others. But for most of us, the financial motivation is low on the list of reasons for becoming our own bosses. In a recent discussion among six reasonably successful woman business owners, all of us admitted we'd be earning more in a staff position at a large company—but were much happier running our own firms.

Myth #3. You can avoid office politics. To some extent, this is true—there are certainly no office politics in my immediate workplace. But anyone who has every been called in as a consultant has bumped into the client firm's internal politics, sometimes very uncomfortably.

Myth #4. You'll work fewer hours. To me, this is the wildest dream of all. Most new entrepreneurs put in longer hours than they'd ever imagined—or wanted. Making a business grow takes a real commitment of time and energy, and a home-based business is so nearby that it never quite leaves you. It seems that just a couple of hours on the weekend will make next week's workload so much easier . . . or, if I just work on the books after the kids are asleep, I won't have any interruptions. When your own earnings are tied to your output, you may suddenly feel impelled to keep at it.

Myth #5. You won't have to take orders. Certainly no one will be standing over you all day telling you what to do, but ask anyone who has ever had a customer if she takes orders. For the amount of time you are dealing with any client, each one of them is your boss. He or she is hiring you, specifying the service he or she wants you to provide, paying you, and evaluating your performance. And let's face it, if you're not "taking orders" from someone, you're not selling anything.

Myth #6. (For night owls only.) You can sleep late. When I quit my last full-time job, I was, frankly, looking forward to leisurely mornings, waking up at 10:00 A.M. Harsh reality descended remarkably quickly: just because I had altered my work life, the city's business community had not changed in any way. It was still operating from 9:00 A.M. to

5:00 P.M. If I wanted to sleep through the first phone calls of the day, and field others before my second cup of coffee, I had that option, but it soon seemed an unwise tactic. People who phone at 9:01 A.M. are frequently hard to reach for the rest of the day, and though I was perky at 8:00 P.M., it's a tough time to return business calls. (Creative professionals are free to work at any hour, but if you have to interact with the rest of the world, it's best to be functional by 9:00 A.M.!)

Myth #7. You can be with your baby while you work. Experts I know are adamant on this point. Kathleen Lewis, who founded her child-care company when her daughter was a baby, learned firsthand that she couldn't simultaneously be a mother and a businesswoman. "If you're going to run a home-based business, and you want to take it seriously, you have to arrange for the same kind of child care you would if you went to work for an employer. No one can pay attention to a baby and a client at the same time," Lewis maintains.

Well into my second decade as a business owner, I made a long, personal list of entrepreneurship's pluses and minuses. Most are shared by other women entrepreneurs I've met:

PLUSES
- *Autonomy.* You're in charge! No one is going to tell you what to do all day or how to use your time.
- *Variety.* You'll probably find a wide range among the tasks you have to perform and the kinds of clients for whom you'll work.
- *Total responsibility.* The buck stops (and starts) with you.
- *No staff meetings.* If you're eager to cross these off your to-do lists, sole proprietorship will satisfy your wish.
- *No interoffice memos.* Did you hate the time you had to spend reading, routing, writing, and responding to interoffice communiqués while you had a staff job? You'll relish deleting them from your existence. (I must confess, after all these years, I rarely stop

to count this particular blessing, but it was a great joy the first six months!)

+ *No rush-hour commuting.* Hearing the traffic reports, in the comfort of my dining room, I never fail to appreciate the thirty-second commute to my sunny, fully equipped office.

+ *Setting your own structure.* If you're highly motivated and prefer planning the way you use your time, you'll love being your own boss. Self-employment is perfect for self-starters. People often tell me I must be very disciplined. Discipline has nothing to do with it. When you notice the connection between food/clothing/shelter and sitting down to work each day, a built-in incentive program takes root.

+ *Excitement.* A new small business is automatically unpredictable. Consumer habits, trends, and the vagaries of the marketplace can also be quirky. If you like the idea of never being complacent or certain of how things are going, you'll enjoy the thrill of ownership.

+ *The ability to branch out at will.* A benefit of running your own show is having the flexibility to add on a new service or product, as the market dictates. You can opt to learn a new skill and fold it into the mix your firm offers.

+ *The freedom to choose co-workers (and, to some extent, clients).* Since you're the boss, you can hire the part- or full-time employees you wish to have around you. I always make sure they are people whose presence is a positive part of my workday. While I've been fortunate in recruiting very good part-time helpers, I choose to have them work in their own home offices, rather than in mine, and I can schedule meetings with them as often as I wish. The benefit of selecting clients is not so available to brand-new entrepreneurs. As you get under way, you may realize some prospects sound like more trouble than they could possibly be worth. It's a wonderful feeling to know that your financial survival does not depend on saying yes to everyone who calls.

- *The opportunity to work at home.* Some of us love it; others find it unbearable. Your own business is the ideal home-office situation, allowing you to set up a convenient space to match your needs perfectly.

- *Shifting your office with the seasons.* If you have a deck, a garden, a patio, or other outdoor space, you may be able to take advantage of today's technology and spend some of your work time outside. With a cordless phone or a laptop, I can block out an hour for telephone calls on my brownstone terrace on warm afternoons. At our country house, I have a rolling computer cart that wheels out onto the deck (overlooking a babbling brook in the woods), and in good weather I keep Mondays free of appointments to stay outside writing.

- *Taking a break when you need it.* When a heavy deadline is staring at you, frivolity is inappropriate. But under normal circumstances, you can probably give yourself a regenerative time-out at the point in the day when you would most benefit. I've loved being able to free an hour to suit up, stretch, and run three or four miles, five days a week. I can't always manage it at my favorite time, the end of the workday, since weather or daylight may interfere, but I find it so energizing and head-clearing that I always return raring to get back to work. Some of my most creative solutions to client problems have come about while I was jogging.

Yet, all is not paradise, even for the most happily self-employed. Here are some of the negatives:

MINUSES

- *Isolation.* One of my friends, a career civil servant, left her job with a city agency to start a small business. The firm did well, but she was unhappy and soon went back to her old job. When I asked why, she said simply, "I missed gossip." I knew what she meant: not malicious, harmful backstabbing, but just the friendly, grapevine exchange of life's little tidbits with people one sees every day. It gets lonely working by yourself all day long, and my friend recognized her preference for company on coffee breaks and lunches.

* *Risk.* Even though you or I will do everything in our power to ensure survival, no one can guarantee you that our businesses will be there next year.

* *Feast-or-famine syndrome.* Running your own business, whatever the field, brings ups and downs. I often describe it as an emotional and financial roller coaster.

* *No one to whom to delegate.* Especially if you were good at turning tasks over to others, it's hard to accept doing everything your-self—unless or until you pay someone else a salary to do some of those jobs for you.

* *No paid benefits.* Say good-bye to paid vacations, sick days, company-reimbursed tuition, and your employer's health insu-rance. (The flip side of this factor, I've discovered, is that self-employment cures everything from menstrual cramps to the common cold!)

* *No colleagues or feedback.* You can't ask anyone to take a look at something you've just done or listen to an idea. You have to learn to shift gears or take a break and then evaluate your own work with a degree of objectivity.

* *No guaranteed income.* You'll reap what you've sown.

* *You play all the roles.* I like being president. I don't like being janitor. Everything in between is mine, too.

Preventive Steps

I'd like to share some ways to avoid three of the difficulties I labeled "minuses": isolation, benefits, and delegating. To contain the costs of delegating some of your activities, check into work-study, internship, and co-operative education programs at the nearest high schools, junior colleges, and universities. You may be able to recruit an eager, energetic

student at a very reasonable rate. A badge of achievement offered by
the Girl Scouts through its Gold Award program is another source of
assistance for you. Teenage Girl Scouts do volunteer work in a small
business for a designated number of hours per week, over a two-year
period. The experience helps them learn about business, while earning
a Merit Badge. Contact the nearest Girl Scouts office or chapter for
details. Special incentive programs also encourage business owners to
hire and train handicapped workers. Employers are not required to pay
benefits to people working fewer than twenty hours a week.

Time-Out

Speaking of benefits, I encourage you to take at least a one-week
vacation each year, even though you may sacrifice some income for the
time you're away. We all need to feel we've earned some kind of reward.
When I was a career counselor, I left town for all of August, and
virtually started over again each September, which kept my earnings
low for those two months. My marketing business is much more
lucrative, and I don't wish to give up a month's revenues. I go on
vacation for two weeks before Labor Day, which tends to be a slow time,
and usually the week between Christmas and New Year's, when almost
no business is transacted in my city.

A few years ago, I found myself manifesting unmistakable—and
unpleasant—symptoms of burnout in March. I realized I needed a rest,
but enough work was piled up that I couldn't see my way out of town
until at least May. After a long internal battle, I admitted my inability
to close my office for even a brief, mental health break meant something
was very wrong with the way I was operating. As long as those days
were blocked out on my calendar way in advance, it should be possible
for me to be away from, say, Wednesday through Friday. Once I'd given
myself permission for a minivacation, chosen dates, and made reser-
vations, I began looking forward to it avidly. Though weeks away, that
carrot of a few days in a quaint, old beach town eased my tension
enormously. With something delicious to look forward to, I could feel

that my hard work would also allow me some special pleasures. Nothing terrible happened because I closed the office for three days, and I accepted the fact that it's a long way from January 1 to mid-August.

Now I ward off burnout each year by scheduling a three-day "spring break," and head for someplace lovely and totally unrelated to work. (Clients are welcome to assume I'm away at a conference.) Though a tough boss, I try not to work on major holidays, so I can feel normal. (Yet, here I am writing this on Washington's Birthday.) I don't take sick days, but that doesn't mean you shouldn't. Somehow, the threat of all that lost income feels worse than whatever minor malady I may be suffering!

Under the American healthcare system, no sane person can go without medical insurance. When I left my last full-time job, the insurance carrier continued to provide my coverage at the group rate, and I payed for it myself each quarter. I did so for years, until I remarried and was covered by the excellent benefits package of my spouse's employer. (Unfortunately, the law now allows coverage to be extended for only eighteen months.) Another way to get medical and other insurance is through a professional association in your industry or an alumni organization at your alma mater. Many of these groups offer insurance plans at group rates.

Home Alone

For me, like many other businesswomen, isolation is the toughest problem of working alone. If you're used to having co-workers around, to share ideas and brainstorm, sole proprietorship is a huge change. These antidotes have helped me over the last fourteen years:

- Make lunch dates with friends. Having some social interaction in the middle of the day is a good change of pace. If it's a former co-worker, you'll have a chance to talk shop with an understanding colleague. It may be hard to spare two hours in midday once you get rolling, so learn to schedule appointments with clients and suppliers to allow for lunch with friends in their vicinity.

- If you're an early riser, set up breakfast dates before friends head for their jobs. The morning conversation will leave you stimulated when you return to your home office. Some entrepreneurs go out to breakfast every morning at the same local diner. They claim it's to get out of the house before settling down to work; I suspect another motive is friendly chitchat with the same daily crowd.

- Take a midday dance or exercise class, if they exist in your community. A recent Purdue University study showed physical activity helps stimulate creative thinking. It's good for you, breaks up your routine, and puts you among other people for part of the day.

- Join local professional associations. The Kiwanis Club, Rotary, chamber of commerce, or small-business group probably has lunch or breakfast meetings. (In addition to the social enjoyment of mingling with other executives, you may also develop some good business leads!)

- Start your own small-business support group. Other sole proprietors are also isolated and will be glad to meet with peers once or twice a month. Put an announcement in the local business publication or at the office supplies store, copy shop, and other places home-based entrepreneurs may be. Ask people you know if any of their neighbors work in home offices. Make a few phone calls to invite them to the first lunch at a specific time and place. It's surprisingly easy to form a small group of business owners. I've done it twice.

- If possible, choose suppliers you like. When I'm hungry for human contact, I'm glad I can drop in at my printer, graphic designer, and stationery store to exchange pleasantries, gripes, or even inane remarks about the weather.

No matter what kind of business you begin, one thing is certain: running it will cause some real changes in the way you live. By anticipating the new circumstances cited in this chapter, and projecting other features in your own situation, you'll be able to plan ahead and line up ways to surmount each obstacle. Unexpected events can be unsettling, but if you take the time to organize your approaches to the major shifts in your day-to-day life, you will probably be able to stay on an even keel.

~

Before You Begin: Preliminary Steps

$\mathscr{S}$o far, you're eager to become a business owner and you have a reasonable idea of a service you'd like to offer. The next steps involve some serious time and effort on your part—which is excellent practice for entrepreneurship—because this is when you begin solidifying your goals. What do you do first? Homework.

Research Your Field

Your first activity is to head for the nearest business library. In cities, one branch of the public library system usually has a substantial business section. In smaller communities, try to arrange access to the campus library of a college that offers business courses, or plan to spend a day in the nearest city that has the material you need. The World Wide Web can also be an excellent source for this kind of information. A number of the reference books mentioned below are also available online.

Research Clues

What are you trying to find out? Everything you can about the field you're considering, including:

- How many people are involved in this field?
- Is it suited to self-employment?
- What are the average earnings?
- Is special training required? If so, what kind?
- Is the field growing?
- How many prospective customers will you have?
- What sort of equipment or material is needed?
- Does the industry have a professional association?
- Is it a seasonal business?
- What are the important issues in the field today?
- What are the typical hours?

Allow a minimum of two hours for your visits. Bring a writing pad and take a lot of notes. An easy starting point may be the *Occupational Outlook Handbook*, published every other year by the U.S. Department of Labor. It gives clear, readable information and projections about thousands of careers. Another introductory source is the *Business Periodicals Index*, which will cite articles on the industry you're exploring. Sit down and read all the material you can get your hands on, especially the most recent articles, with their more up-to-date information. One of your goals at the business library is to learn some of the buzzwords in the field, if you don't already know them.

To find out the professional associations in the field, check the *Encyclopedia of Associations* and write down every organization related to the service you have in mind. You'll also want to identify the trade publications geared to this kind of business, which may not be included in the *Business Periodicals Index*. Ask for any major directories of periodicals, which are arranged by subject.

Making the business librarian your ally will save you a lot of time and effort. Simply tell the staff member which business you're re-searching; he or she will usually suggest sources to consult.

Depending on the resources available to you, you may be able to spend a productive half day at a business library every week for a few months. If you're exploring a field about which not much is written (such as an errand or tutoring service), you'll probably get through your library's material fairly quickly.

In either case, your research has barely begun, for you can turn to many other sources. Here are some potential information providers and the type of data each might furnish:

* *The local chambers of commerce.* These groups often have general business facts about the community and may run special-interest programs for different types of businesses.

* *Trade or professional associations.* Most of these organizations keep national data about their industry. Many take salary and other surveys of their members, and publish periodicals on topics of interest. If you can't locate a chapter in your region, contact the national headquarters. Someone will be able to steer you to the nearest branch. Start going to meetings as soon as your research makes you comfortable with the notion of being in this field.

* *The nearest Economic Development Agency (EDA).* Check the telephone book or business sections of the local paper for news about which state, county, and private not-for-profit agencies take an interest in helping community residents start small businesses. They are likely to keep statistics on new business start-ups and demographic data about what kinds of consumers live in the area. Call them, ask how you can get copies of their data, and find out what types of assistance they offer. By the way, as soon as you know what enterprise you're going to launch, make an appoint-ment to meet with someone at the EDA office.

* *Banks and realtors in the community where you expect to run your business.* They're always taking the economic pulse of their service

area, so they have today's information about the types of people that are moving into (or out of) your target area. Bankers approve the mortgages and Realtors sell the properties, so these professionals know the income levels, household compositions, and socioeconomic details about buyers and sellers. In fairness to busy professionals, be judicious in the way you take up someone's time. Turn first to a loan officer at the bank where you have an account or a mortgage. He or she will be glad to hear you're planning to start a business, as this may mean another account at the bank. Similarly, if you bought your house from a local broker, visit him or her at a weekday hour when customers are not around. Realtors, also, like to learn about new businesses in the neighborhood, for that could mean you'll need to rent office space. (You don't have to interview both a real estate broker and a banker, but the more information you collect, the more knowledgeable you become about your target community.)

◆ *The U.S. Small Business Administration (SBA).* The SBA publishes a huge assortment of nominally priced leaflets on all sorts of small-business topics. Contact the nearest office of the SBA for a list of all the publications currently available. You can find the listing in the Government Blue Pages of your telephone directory, or call the SBA's toll-free number (800-8-ASK-SBA). Some of its literature is excellent; all of it is reasonably priced.

As you do your research, you'll probably be refining the focus of your business to match your findings. One of the most crucial questions you'll have to answer is: Does my community need this service? "Community" in this context may refer to either a geographic area or a particular segment of the market. A good way to find out is by checking what is already available, so it's time to:

Study the Competition

An easy way to see who else is in the field is to look in the local Yellow Pages. While exploring the prospects for her future career counseling firm, one of my clients checked the Yellow Pages in her city and found ten career advisement listings. She called each one to request information. They all sent a brochure or sales kit, giving her a great head start on knowing what was available to her prospective clients. Are you uncomfortable calling a business to get information under false pretenses? I have two suggestions:

- ask a relative or friend to make one call for you
- accept the reality that this is standard business practice

Once you're operating, competitors will covertly call you, too!

To see who else offers the service or product you hope to provide, visit all the trade shows where current competitors may be exhibiting their wares. Talk to salespeople. Read their literature. Pay attention to what each company stresses as the advantages of buying its products or services. Check out visitors, too, as you walk around. What seem to be the most frequent concerns? Are sales being made or is business sluggish?

Salespeople and suppliers are great sources of information. Call the companies you would buy from when you get started and meet with sales reps. Take the time to find out what they could provide you with on your anticipated budget, and the payment terms they'll be able to offer. While discussing your projected needs, ask about the state of the industry. Are your competitors thriving or starving? No one knows better what's happening to his or her customers than a sales rep.

Do your own market research. Call people you know who fit the profile of your target customer. Ask them what they look for when they buy this kind of product or service, how much they're willing to spend, how often they need it, and from whom they currently buy it. You can also recruit business majors from a nearby college to do some shopper surveys for you, for a nominal fee. They stop consumers in heavily trafficked locations and ask a few well-chosen questions. Enlisting a professor to make your research a class project would be ideal. (You can also buy detailed reports from market research companies. Though expensive for a $2,000 budget, the information is thorough and timely. Reports from FIND/SVP, a major supplier, start at $500. Call 800-346-3787 to receive its catalog.)

If you know anyone who has ever worked for a competitor, he or she can tell you a lot about the way the business operates, who the customers are, and what sort of complaints or problems arise. Are any of your competitors publicly owned companies? Then they have to file documents with the Securities and Exchange Commission as well as, in some states, annual statements of condition. You can also purchase a Dun & Bradstreet report about their credit rating. Be sure to read all the trade publications your competitors get. They'll clue you in on trends, issues, and difficulties in the field.

Finally, if you're considering a product, buy the one each of your competitors offers. Take them apart! Do a very careful study of everything about them, including the package and directions. Diligent research is one of the most effective things a new entrepreneur can do to ensure success.

Find Your Niche

Unless you've created a brand-new business, never before offered, you'll have to compete for customers against more established firms. To convince people to buy from you, you will have to show them how your product or service will give them more advantages than that offered by anyone else.

To do that, sit down and study all your research findings to identify a way you can be different from the competition. Your goal is to provide a feature that makes you unique in your field. Here are some possible factors that might become your Unique Selling Proposition (U.S.P.):

- *A feature of the product itself.* Yours could be the only sport sock with built-in magnets, so that keys will stick to it during athletic activities.

- *An aspect of your service.* One of my clients, a small home-based ad agency, promoted weekend and overnight service as their specialty. Naturally, most of their calls came on Friday afternoons or Christmas Eve, but they found it a perfect way to get their feet in the doors of desirable firms.
- *Your target customer (market niche).* Declare that your firm specializes in a particular type of client, and you will attract their notice. I had no trouble positioning my company as the experts in marketing for graphic artists (but eventually learned this was too narrow a segment).
- *Your area of expertise.* Is your background in a very specific or unusual area? If you're about to become the only computer consultant in your city who worked at Apple for a decade, that will make you the Macintosh expert. Capitalize on your unsurpassed firsthand knowledge.

When you've reached the point of identifying a U.S.P. for your business, you've come a long way toward getting it started. Now translate your idea into a twenty-five-word statement of what your company will do:

My business will _____

_____

_____

Once you can do that, you're ready to:

Draft a Business Plan

I promise to make this a totally unintimidating experience—if you promise not to skip this section! Entrepreneurs who are seeking outside financing, a partner, venture capital, or any kind of investor have to put together a formal business plan. Even if your initial funds come from your savings, this is a wonderful exercise for anyone launching any new enterprise. You can buy entire books on writing a comprehensive business plan, but for your $2,000 start-up, all you need to get on paper is a description of how your firm is going to operate and earn a profit.

Since you probably won't be showing your plan to anyone, it doesn't need complicated charts, tables, or graphs. You can even handwrite it. The plan will be useful when you're talking with potential suppliers, organizing your start-up tasks, setting up the office, arranging your schedule, and launching your first promotion efforts.

Begin your business plan by making an outline of all the information you accumulated during the research phase. You'll see exactly where the gaps in your investigation have been, allowing you to fill them effectively.

I devised a simple approach, based on the "Five Ws" you may remember from high school English classes. Writing out the answers to each question in this outline will give you a basic, but perfectly adequate, business plan: What is the exact nature of your business? Here you can expand a little on that twenty-five-word definition.

- *Who is your prototypical customer?* How many of them are in your target community? What do you know about them? And who will be running your business? How much experience or knowledge of the field does the owner have? What are the assets, contacts, and resources the owner brings to the business?
- *Where will this business operate?* If it's in your home, how will the office be set up and equipped? What are the advantages (and disadvantages) of the location?
- *When will you launch your business?* How do you anticipate it will grow?
- *Why does your community (or target market) need your business?* What will you offer that the competition doesn't? Explain how your firm will be unique.
- *How do you plan to advertise and promote your business?* When will these marketing efforts begin?
- *How much?* Outline a budget of projected operating expenses and

anticipated income. Use realistic figures, based on your research, especially of competitors.

Once you've organized your research material and filled in any missing information, add the details to your outline, in any readable form. A business plan can follow any logical format, as long as it provides all the needed information.

Drafting your business plan will show you just what you need to know or do to get started. Ironically, when I wrote a business plan for my second company (on a yellow legal pad), I could see where the gap was: right in the "how" section (advertising and promotion). I didn't have a clear enough idea of how to reach my target customers. By seeing this hole in my plan, I was able to seek assistance in developing a marketing strategy appropriate to my budget. (Chapter 13 will detail just where to get expert help when you need it.)

How to Choose a Name for Your Business

Selecting company names is a big business in America. High-priced consulting firms converted International Harvester into Navistar and American Can into Primerica, among many other name changes of the late eighties. You don't need a consultant to choose your business name, but it does require long and careful thought.

Companies in some fields, such as law and accounting, traditionally use partners' names as their titles. An artistic field, however, invites creative phrases. Here are some pointers for choosing a business name:

1. *Make it something people can remember.* This is what fixes your firm in the public's mind.
2. *Keep it easy to spell!* If a consumer can't find you in the phone book and can't give the information operator an exact spelling, you just lost a prospective sale.
3. *A name should communicate the service or product you offer.* For example, my client Pinch Sitters provides short-term temporary child care. Another client, SMOKE-FREE (a division of Health

Management Consultants), helps people to stop smoking. Brown-stone Graphics offers personalized stationery featuring a pen-and-ink portrait of the customer's home. The Arbor Barber is a tree surgeon and landscaper.

4. *Great names draw positive attention.* Lick Your Chops produces natural foods for dogs. Many Happy Returns is a storefront tax-preparation shop. Someday My Prints Will Come does mail-order film processing. These are catchy, memorable names.

5. *Convey the image you want to create.* A store in my neighborhood, Made by U.S., sells only American crafts. One of my students named her crafts shop Folks' Art. You have to feel comfortable with the name, since that's how you'll be presenting yourself to the public.

6. *Don't limit yourself with your name.* If you're doing soup-to-nuts catering, Susie's Great Desserts undersells your scope. Similarly, don't impose geographic restrictions. Once you choose Georgetown Word Processors as the name, calls from other sections of greater Washington, D.C., become less likely.

The name can reveal what's unique about your business. Only Hearts, a Manhattan boutique, stocks nothing but items with hearts on them. Tennis Lady sells sporting togs for women. I shop at DownTown for warm winter garments.

You can choose a name by focusing on your location, the size of your company, your particular product or service, or by a witty play on words. Excellent names I've encountered include Blazing Salads (a Greenwich Village restaurant), Taskmasters (an errand service), Mathworks (a fear-of-math program), and First Impressions (image consulting). For some reason, outstanding business tags often belong to caterers, whose appealing, clever names imply these firms will be equally imaginative and memorable with food. Among my favorites are A La Carte, The Moveable Feast, Dutch Treats, and Glorious Food. Sometimes, my start-up clients ask for help naming their companies; I'm proud to have christened Burke's Bytes (a word-processing firm owned by Kathleen Burke) and Career Power (a career consulting firm).

Can a name really make a difference? Financial consultant Louise Davida, then at Gruntal & Co., became the instructor of an established New York University course, Charting the Commodities Market. Several years later, she renamed the course How to Tame and Trade the Commodities Futures Market. Registration quadrupled!

A word of warning: you can't use a name that belongs to another business. When I finally settled on the perfect name for my marketing communications firm, a check of the telephone directory revealed a downtown employment agency was already called Business Builders. (That's how I became Milano Marketing, which certainly says what we do and is easy to remember, but is not as powerful as my original choice.) Chapter 8 will provide the details on how to find out if you will be allowed to use the name you've selected.

Test It Part Time

Before you quit your job and plunge full-speed-ahead into your new business, I'd like to offer a more prudent and gradual approach. The optimal way to determine if your business is feasible is to test it on a part-time basis.

Frankly, while this is great advice, it doesn't always work. In many cases, it is really impossible to explore the concept you've come up with while you have a full-time job. Of course, if your company lays off four thousand people (including you) or relocates to another part of the country, you have nothing to lose by devoting your efforts to a new enterprise while looking for a job.

The part-time test works best if your new venture can operate on evenings and weekends. Some fields lend themselves to this readily: wedding photography, résumé writing, any type of mail-order business, calligraphy, word processing, dressmaking, plant care for out-of-town professionals, tutoring, etc. With a business of this nature, you can implement your promotional plans on a modest basis and see what kind of response you get. Remember not to take on more than you can handle in the time available! What you do not need are frustrated customers griping about your slow service. If demand is there, and you see real potential for repeat or new business, the evidence suggests you have a viable idea.

Many other fields do not make sense on an evening/weekend basis, especially if your prospects are business executives who expect to meet with you during traditional working hours. To test an idea under these circumstances, you may want to set up a part-time employment situation. Erica Gjersvik prepared herself to run Pangaea by working several days a week at a crafts shop selling items imported from Mexico, while setting up her own venture the rest of the time. She had some daytime hours free for meeting with prospective buyers. (Aside from the stable income, she learned a lot by working for an existing company!)

Consultants can sometimes get started by shifting to a three- or four-day week at their current employer. How much you want to tell your company about your future plans should be determined by its needs and policies. Is it promoting early retirement because profits are down? Your company will probably be glad you're seeking a cut in pay. Conversely, if your department is understaffed and you're one of the senior people, your company won't want to have you around less.

The part-time approach is perfect if you're at home with a small child. By taking small steps into the entrepreneurial pond, you'll soon be able to see if it's deep enough for a serious swim. Every customer will be a learning experience. One of the best aspects of testing a new business part time is the chance it gives the owner to see if she likes what she'd be doing all day.

Eight Ways to See If Your Business Idea Is Viable

Before you quit your job and open your new enterprise, take these steps to make sure you've identified a business that can succeed in your area.

1. See if you can test it on a part-time basis, to get a sense of what attracts people and how much they're willing to pay for your product or service.

2. Work for an established firm in this type of business long enough to see what is really involved on a day-to-day basis. It's crucial for you to like the activities you'd be performing. (Volunteer for a few hours a week if you can't get anyone to pay you.)

3. If you're considering a product, rent a booth at a community fair or block party. Chat at length with everyone who stops by, and eavesdrop on comments of people who don't. This is inexpensive, wonderful market research.

4. Call sales reps at the companies that supply the industry you're considering. You need to know their prices as you plan your budget, and they can tell you about market conditions in their territory. Listen carefully for news of problems.

5. Talk to a realtor and a banker in the community where you want to base your business. Both of these professionals monitor the economic pulse of their community carefully and can tell you what kinds of consumers and commercial firms are moving in—or out.

6. Go through the Yellow Pages to see where the existing competitors are. Call or visit as many of them as you can. Who are their customers? What are their main selling points? How is business?

7. Check with the nearest local development corporation or Economic Development Agency. These groups track business development in their target areas and can give you valuable information about what types of businesses are opening or closing.

8. Get data from the U.S. Small Business Administration and the professional associations in the particular field you're considering. They may have materials that tell you what size population is needed to support your kind of business. You can match this information against marketplace data from the local chamber of commerce.

～

CHAPTER EIGHT

Getting Down to Business

ow that you've gone through all the explorations and outlined a basic plan for making your business idea a reality, this chapter details the steps you need to follow to get started.

Setting Up an Office

In order to qualify for a tax deduction, the space you set aside for your business has to be exclusively used for that purpose. This is easiest to accomplish if you can choose a separate room or at least clearly partition a specific area. In a studio apartment, it's harder to make it clear that your office space is not used for any other activity.

Be honest about your environmental needs. If you're going to be depressed in a windowless workspace, do not choose a spot in the darkest corner of the garage or basement! You won't be productive in an unfriendly setting. Make your office as appealing as possible so that you'll be eager to get to work each day.

Wherever you place your home office, it needs these items:

- a desk and adjustable chair
- a telephone
- a place for files
- space for supplies

Most service businesses require certain types of equipment, typically a word processor and/or a computer. In our high-tech era, many small businesses have copiers and fax machines. These are not essential on day one, unless you live very far from the nearest public fax or copy shops. To contain start-up costs, consider leasing some of your equipment. Illustrators' rep Vicki Morgan, for example, who has been in business for many years, leases her copier. "It's worth it to get a more sophisticated, larger machine, worth $3,500 at the time I first got it," she reflects. The copier costs her about $100 a month, and the leasing company will upgrade as newer equipment becomes available. "You're not stuck with a dinosaur," Morgan remarks. "With technology changing at such a rapid pace, it may make more sense to lease, especially with an option to buy, for a nominal cost. When I spent $5,000 on a copier, I was miserable. Leasing is probably a better way to deal with a start-up budget."

Morgan also leases her telephones. "A new phone system was going to cost me $2,500, and I didn't have the cash to lay out," she explains. "This way I can change phones at any time. They repair it at no cost— they fix it because you're leasing it. I don't have to worry about the equipment now."

When she started out, Morgan bought secondhand furnishings, such as flat files, and recommends checking used office-furniture stores for good buys.

If you expect to hire helpers, think about where they can work. Is your office area big enough for an employee? Will you be able to add equipment or storage space as your business grows? Try not to lock yourself into a cramped, finite corner.

With so many home businesses now operating, manufacturers are creating all sorts of products to help us set up efficient workplaces in small spaces. Reliable Home Office, a huge mail-order firm, specializes in products for the home-based entrepreneur. Its catalogs will give you good ideas about how to arrange your office and terrific suggestions of useful items to put in it.

Be sure to shop around for your equipment and supply purchases. Prices can vary enormously. If you know what you want, check with the nearest used office-furniture dealers. Unless customers will be coming to your office, you do not need expensive, cutting-edge furnishings. Check the wares at a reputable computer exchange for good deals or last year's models. Sometimes mail-order companies offer very competitive prices on standard items, particularly during sales. The Quill Corporation, for example, may be a good source for many of your requirements. Since the mid-nineties, discount office-supply chain stores, such as OfficeMax and Staples, have been spreading throughout the country. If there is a store like this in your area, it may be a convenient and inexpensive place to acquire your basics.

That covers the physical aspects, which are pretty straightforward. Here are two key internal requirements you will have to deal with: self-discipline and interruptions. To leap the first obstacle, I urge you to set up a realistic schedule and stick to it. You're the boss, so choose hours that are comfortable and realistic for you. Without a time clock or supervisor watching you, it takes inner commitment to punch in every morning. The easiest way to train yourself to get to the office is to declare the hours your business will be operating, whether it's 9:00 A.M. to 5:00 P.M., 10:00 A.M. to 6:00 P.M., 9:00 A.M. to 9:00 P.M., 8:00 A.M. to 7:00 P.M., or noon to 3:00 P.M. By telling people the times you can be reached in your office, you're planting your own motivation to be there.

Conversely, if you don't decide and declare your hours of operation, it's all too easy, especially in your start-up days, to let other activities keep you from getting down to business. Another difficulty you may face when you start your home-based enterprise is phone calls from friends and relatives, who misinterpret being at home to mean you're free to talk to them during the day.

You can control these interruptions by showing seriousness and consistency about your new business. Once friends and family see your determination to succeed, they won't intrude on your work time. It's up to you to send a clear message. Be sure you notify all your cronies and relatives of the official opening of your new enterprise, and explain clearly what it is that you're doing. Give yourself a title, like president or director.

The way you answer the phone delivers a message. A crisp "Wizard Word Processing, can I help you?" will sound like you mean business. However, saying "Hello" as if you're at home makes it hard for the caller to know you're a business owner.

Avoid the temptation to chat for half an hour when you get a call between 9:00 A.M. and 5:00 P.M. You can easily "train" friends who call during standard business hours by politely saying, "I'm with a client right now. Can I call you tonight?" or "I'm working on a rush job. I'll get back to you later." When callers hear this once or twice, they'll quickly learn to ask, "Are you in the middle of something?" when they have to phone during your office hours.

In a brand-new enterprise, when you work alone, social phone calls are a tempting distraction. If you're serious about building a successful business, let your friends and family help you. Instead of chatting on the phone, arrange to meet for lunch. Share your business goals with the people who care about you. Let them offer suggestions and encouragement. Give them some business cards or promotional pieces they can pass on to anyone in need of your service. Getting out of your office for an hour and exchanging ideas is an important antidote to the isolation of working alone.

At the beginning, you may welcome interruptions because you may not have much work. Building a stream of clients takes time, so use your free hours for promotional activities. When you're committed to and wrapped up in your business, people will understand—and want to hear about it. Being your own boss is a popular American fantasy. Give your friends the crucial role of referral sources and support system. Once clients keep you busy, you'll automatically limit personal calls because you really won't have time for them.

One additional note for your home office: get dressed. A home-based publicist once told me people actually ask her, "Do you work in a robe?" Needless to say, when you meet with clients, you'll be wearing the same type of attire they are. But if yours is the kind of service where you see clients only rarely, you'll have no firm reason to put on a pin-striped suit or tailored dress every morning. I've known people who found they just didn't sound businesslike on the phone unless they were dressed like the executives they were calling. I think it's fine to wear casual, comfortable clothes when you work at home—my typical office uniform is a brightly colored sweatsuit in winter, a T-shirt dress in summer—but you certainly will feel and sound more professional when you take the time to put on real clothes and makeup.

Register Your Business

Before your first customer arrives, register the name of your business if you do not simply plan to operate under your own legal name. The registration procedure varies from state to state. If you haven't set up a partnership arrangement, your category will be sole proprietor. After registering, you'll receive a d/b/a (doing business as) certificate, which legally allows you to operate under your business name.

In California, the county clerk's office handles d/b/a certificates. After the owner fills out the appropriate form and pays the filing fee, she is then required to publish the business name and principal owner of the firm for four consecutive weeks in a classified ad in any news-paper (for which the newspaper will bill her directly). After four weeks, it's presumed that no one is contesting use of the name this business has chosen. In Pennsylvania, the Department of State handles small-business registration. A sole proprietor initiates the process with a phone call to the Corporation Bureau in Harrisburg, where an employee checks the name of the new business for availability. If the name is not in use, the bureau sends all the necessary forms to the new owner, who completes and returns them by mail.

It takes a few phone calls to discover the registration steps in any state. Using the Blue Pages of your telephone book, start by calling either the county clerk or the information number for the county executive office.

Here's a shortcut, with a bonus: the U.S. Small Business Administration sponsors SCORE (the Service Corps of Retired Executives), with chapters all over the country. At your local SCORE office, a seasoned businessperson can give you all the specifics on exactly how to register a new business in your state. The bonus: you can also make an appointment for free counseling and get answers to other questions you may have. For the SCORE office nearest you, access SCORE information at the SBA's toll-free number: 800-8-ASK-SBA.

Here are three strong reasons to register your new business:

* It will make you feel more like an owner when you get that certificate.
* With your d/b/a certificate, you can open a separate bank account in your business name.
* You'll be able to get a telephone for your business.

Obtain Permits or Licenses

In some places, certain types of businesses require a permit or license. While you were doing your research, you probably came across this information. When you track down the registration procedure in your state, ask each person who gives you information if the type of business you plan to start requires any kind of permit or license. That will assure you of finding the most up-to-date legal requirements.

In my state, licenses are required for locksmiths, employment agencies, bakeries, notaries, real estate brokers, hairdressers, private investigators, and cosmetologists, among other fields.

If you plan to hire anyone to help you, on a part-time or freelance basis, get an employer I.D. number. The nearest Internal Revenue Service (IRS) office will supply you with one, at no charge. You'll also need this number to open a business bank account. (The IRS office will be listed in the Blue Pages of your local telephone book.)

Get Business Cards and Letterhead

When you open your door for business, you need cards and letterhead on hand. Here's good news for that $2,000 budget: only if you're in an image business or offer a very high-end service do you need to spend a significant amount on what my profession calls "corporate identity materials." Otherwise, for start-up needs, head for a copy shop or stationery store that has big sample books of predesigned business cards and letterhead. You choose the style, typeface, and ink color you want, write out the details, and wait for your order to be delivered. Because these mass-production firms deal in huge volume, they can keep costs very low for standard items. A minimum order is usually five hundred cards. Black ink on white paper is the least expensive choice, and, again, perfectly okay as long as yours is not an image-oriented or expensive service.

As your business grows and you develop a stronger sense of how you want clients to think of you, you'll probably want professional input to create materials that present your company in exactly the way you want it to be seen.

Announce Yourself

As soon as you set a date to open, send an attractive announcement to everyone you've ever met. The announcement should reflect the way you want people to think of your business: accessible, affordable, elegant, sophisticated, friendly, upscale, down-homey, or whatever. Be sure to convey exactly what service you are providing, so people will know when to think of your company. Referrals, the best way to build a service business, come from the most unexpected places. Put all your relatives, neighbors, ex-classmates, other parents at the day-care center, and former co-workers on your mailing list. The more people that know what service you're offering, the likelier you are to get recommendations. Try to send five hundred announcements.

You don't have to spend a fortune on your announcements (though, unfortunately, postage is costly), but don't skip them, either. They are the most effective way to spread the word about your new business. Even if they're not expensive, they should look professional, so people will take you seriously. You can begin establishing a consistent presence for your business: if you're introducing a creative service, show imagination in your announcement. If it's an image business, be sure your taste and style are reflected. Are you offering typesetting, graphic design, or desktop publishing? Make your announcement a sample of your best work.

Setting Your Prices

As soon as you open for business, people will ask your prices, so have them firmly in mind. I've heard many different approaches to pricing and found most of them confusing. The method that makes the most sense to me is one professional organizations in creative fields often suggest to their members. Here is my interpretation.

Determine what your type of service, at your level of experience, would be worth in your community if you worked full time for an employer. (And be honest here!) Then divide that annual salary by 50 (weeks), because most employers would give you a two-week vacation. Now you've established your weekly worth. Employees presumably work 40 hours each week, but as your own boss, about one-quarter to one-third of your time will be for unbillable tasks like administration, selling, sending invoices, etc. So divide your weekly salary by 28 (hours). This gives you a reasonable basis for calculating what your efforts are worth each hour.

I'd like to stress here that this hourly value is your own private information. Don't share it with your customers. All you tell them is the total price, which we have not yet arrived at.

Now calculate your operating costs. Look back at your business plan notes, and see what you've allocated for all the expenses of running your business. These include advertising, equipment, supplies, postage, messengers, telephone, and everything else you'll deduct on next year's Schedule C when you file your taxes. If you're in a service business, this is a very straightforward calculation. If you're selling a product, be sure to thoroughly research what you'll be paying for all your raw materials and delivery charges. You'll be estimating in the beginning, but by the end of your first year, your records will show you exactly what all these overhead costs were. Divide the annual total by 1,400 (50 weeks times 28 hours, until you have more precise figures on your actual billable hours per year). Add this amount to that hourly figure you calculated in the last step.

Having taken into account the current value of your own labor and the projected operating costs of running your business, you have one more step before arriving at your price—and this is the good one. Aside from all the inner rewards, never forget that you are in business to earn a profit, and it has to be included in your pricing—or you won't have one! You can figure your early profits at 10 to 20 percent above your costs and add that to the fee basis you've arrived at so far.

For a service business, I recommend stating a project price, rather than an hourly rate, whenever possible. I learned a long time ago that clients wanted to know, "What's it going to cost me?" more than how much I was charging them per hour. They needed to fit my services into their budgets; suspense about the final bill made them nervous. By keeping careful track of all the work I did, I soon learned how long it usually took me to do a typical assignment, such as writing a brochure or a one-page sales letter. Once I knew how many hours I could anticipate spending on such a project, I was able to arrive at a fee with which I felt comfortable and which I would use for any new clients. Luckily for me, I'm a very fast writer and often find an assignment takes less time than I'd scheduled. (In all honesty, the big variable may not be my own facility, but the degree of difficulty a particular client offers.)

The good news is that on some projects where the client was cooperative and asked for little rewriting, I earned $90 or $100 an hour, instead of the $50 on which I'd based my calculation. On the other hand, once in a while a project is so difficult or disaster-ridden that it takes far longer than average, and I earn less than I wanted. The balance is clearly in my favor, though, or I would revise my assessment of how long a certain type of work will take.

Some employers will want you to state an hourly rate, and you do need to have one if you provide a service. Another important factor about pricing is to know what comparable products or services currently sell for in your market segment. And before you decide what to charge, you have to find out what the market will bear.

One of my cousins, who has an M.B.A. and a young son, recently launched a hand-painted children's clothing business in partnership with another full-time mother. I expected her to succeed—she certainly had the right background. A few months later, when I asked how the business was going, she told me it had seemed very successful. Parents in her upscale suburban area loved the clothes, but she and her partner had to give up the business because they were not earning a profit. I was perplexed. My cousin explained that their labor-intensive clothes allowed for very limited production, so they couldn't order enough supplies to get volume discounts. With the costs of the basic materials and all the pricey frills they were adding on, she and her partner were just breaking even. "I know you learned in business school that you have to charge enough to cover your labor and your supplies and allow a little profit, too, right?" I asked. She agreed, but advised me there's a limit to what even affluent mothers will spend on a T-shirt. The numbers just didn't work out.

Often when people start out they try to make themselves competitive on price, by charging lower rates than their more established competitors. This may work to your advantage, by bringing in new customers eager for a bargain. Before you try the low-price promotion strategy, though, make sure this is the kind of image you want to create.

Pricing is a critical part of any business's survival, and I have provided only a very brief overview since that is not the focus of this book. I urge you, though, to seek some individual guidance in setting your prices. Two of the best sources are workshops on pricing, presented by many professional associations, or one-to-one consultations offered by programs of the U.S. Small Business Administration, at no charge. (See chapter 12 for more details on resources.)

Special Problems of the Home Office

All the usual home office hurdles can be overcome with good planning. Home-based business owners often wonder:

➤ *Where to meet clients.* Some customers may prefer to come to your office, but many entrepreneurs worry about whether it's "professional" to see clients at home. With 45 million Americans doing some work at home, a tasteful office/residence has become an acceptable business setting. When I interviewed a very successful graphic designer, he led me through the sunny studio at the front of his house to a small conference room, where industry publications and his many awards lined the walls. Clients are at ease there, largely because the designer's attitude signals, "Of course I choose to work here! Wouldn't you?"

These are some alternatives to seeing clients at home:

1. Find a suitable restaurant in an accessible location. A computer consultant has all his meetings in a venerable downtown bistro during quiet afternoon hours.
2. Rent a small office by the hour, from any professional who uses it mainly evenings and early mornings.
3. Meet clients in their offices.
4. Join a club in your town that offers meeting space during business hours. An arts adviser sees her clients at the Alumni Club of a university where she teaches a course; the gracious atmosphere is well worth the fee.
5. Check classified ads in the real estate and business sections

of the daily newspaper and local business publications to see
if any commercial facilities rent small offices by the hour.

* *How to receive packages.* Does your building have a doorman? Is
someone home at your house during business hours? If not, you
might rent a box at the nearest Mailboxes USA, which is ideal for
home-based companies. Make an arrangement with a nearby
retailer who may be willing to act as your pick-up or drop-off
point in exchange for your services or a modest fee. Can you have
express mail and special deliveries sent to your spouse's office
(assuming he and his support staff don't mind, of course)?

* *Intrusions on family life.* Because clients phone at all hours,
consider a separate phone line you can hook up to an answering
machine. State your office hours very clearly in all your material,
and let the machine take messages outside of business hours. Be
sure your family is supportive of your new enterprise. Do not let
your children answer your business line.

* *Cabin fever.* Commuting from your dining room to your den keeps
you indoors. Find an excuse to get out each day, for a shift of gears
and scenery, to keep you alert and energized. A fund-raising
consultant told me she takes four dance classes a week as her
diversion from working and living in the same apartment. My own
antidote is jogging three miles about five times a week.

In spite of the minor difficulties, many home-based entrepreneurs
wouldn't change their setup for anything. The benefits, including low
overhead, easy commuting, and higher profits, are very appealing.

∼

Fifteen Women Who Love Being Their Own Bosses

*I*n these brief interviews, fifteen women describe their businesses and tell how they started out. Each one began at home, with a minuscule investment, and all but one sells a service. These women embody the suggestions made in *Hers*. Though not all of them set out to run a full-time enterprise, each has succeeded in establishing a business that meets her goals.

Calligrapher

For Felicia Saks, calligraphy, she explains, is "very seasonal. We're busy in summer and spring, for weddings." Her firm, Felicitations, hand-letters poems for Christmas, Valentine's Day, and graduation. It will also hand-letter envelopes, place cards, and certificates. She earned a B.A. in art and later took additional classes in calligraphy. "My art background helps. I can add watercolors to poems," Saks notes. She began Felicitations, a part-time service, by posting hand-lettered cards in banks, super-markets, and other stores in her city and the nearby suburbs.

Saks began her career working for printers, as a graphic designer, and then as a sales representative, which still takes up much of her time. People started calling Felicitations as soon as they saw her cards and ads in local community newspapers. Two years later, she started advertising in the three nearest Yellow Pages books, which required her to get a separate business phone for Felicitations. Customers come from her ads in *Bride's* and her exhibits at wedding shows in the area, in addition to Yellow Pages listings and word of mouth.

She has a showroom where she displays Felicitations's calligraphy. Two or three part-time calligraphers assist Saks when the workload is especially heavy. A convenient benefit of her two professions is that she can arrange the printing of the same invitations for which she's done the calligraphy.

Cleaning Service

Merry Marks started her cleaning company, Dustbusters, by putting five hundred fliers on neighborhood automobiles each weekend. "It was great! The fliers kept our overhead low, and the phones started ringing right away," Marks remembers. The first cleaning crew was her own housekeeper and daughters, who recruited other employees by spreading the word for Marks among their friends and neighbors.

Customers provided their own cleaning supplies. Dustbusters began advertising in free neighborhood weekly newspapers after three months, but didn't need recruitment ads for over a year. "We were bonded immediately, then incorporated later on, for $200." Today, it claims to be the largest cleaning service in its community.

Marks saw a limit to the residential market, though, and became certified as a woman-owned business to gain an advantage when she began bidding on corporate and government projects. Though the bidding process can be cumbersome, these commercial projects are much larger and more profitable, so they have become the focus of the business. Marks secured a sizable one-year contract to clean a state office building and eagerly applied for second-year renewal. Handling commercial accounts has meant hiring a permanent crew, with foreman, so overhead has increased significantly. With her entire payroll now on computer, Marks has a full-time office assistant to handle customer calls and administrative tasks, leaving Marks more time for sales visits, prospecting, networking, and personnel management.

Dustbusters rented two different offices in the neighborhood before moving the business back to the brownstone where Marks and her family live. When their tenant moved, Marks and her husband felt that their savings on overhead and the home-office deductions would more than offset the loss of rental income. She's happier working in a cheery office in her own home, where she can be close to her daughters.

Corporate Gift Buyer

Soon after becoming a mother, Fran Yellen heard that a travel magazine needed souvenir gifts for a Singapore-theme promotional event it was running. She and a neighbor, Margaret Martinez, who has two grown children, had been looking around for a business that wouldn't cost much to start. Martinez's background was in marketing and advertising; Yellen's experience managing three gift showrooms helped them get the account.

"At our age, all of a sudden our friends are in positions to hire us. We got lots of good word of mouth. I knew about the corporate gift business because buyers used to come to our showrooms," Yellen reports. "For example, I realized it was unusual to gift-wrap, so we did it, and impressed our first client, the travel magazine. We didn't have to buy anything to get started."

They began with an answering machine and $25 worth of business cards to get them into showrooms. "We bought samples of ribbon and boxes, so we could show things to clients, which cost about $200. Manufacturers sent us photos of gift items, and we would buy one sample at the retail price to show to our prospective clients. When a corporation chose a gift, we would order two hundred of it," explains Yellen, who handles sales. Since the partners had to pay for half the order in advance, they asked clients to pay half the bill up front, "because it was customized," Yellen notes.

Early profits became a typewriter, designer business cards, and stationery, and bulk-priced ribbons and wrappings. They created samples at wholesale prices. The partners chose their genderless name, J. Wyckoff, to make them seem like a larger company. They also got a separate business phone number. After relying initially on word of mouth, they began to make cold calls for their first Christmas season and started expanding their client base.

Cosmetics Company

"I started with $200—half of it borrowed from my sister," laughs Erica Wilkins, president of a thriving cosmetics firm. With her limited capital, she had a factory produce private label samples of lipstick and nail polish. Her sister, a diplomat's wife, sold the first products in West Africa.

Wilkins invested her early profits in experimenting with eye and lip pencils, then foundation. After commuting back and forth to Africa for a year, she quit her job to enter the American market. Even the Chemists' Society was unable to help in her search for a black chemist. Her hairdresser finally led her to Stenu Robinson, who works closely with her to formulate each Erika product. Robinson was previously with Georgette Klinger Skin Care Laboratories and some private-label cosmetics firms.

"We take each item on the road, testing every product on our sales reps and friends, and then go back to the lab with all their negative and positive feedback. Every product is tested and retested until the consumers love it," Wilkins explains. The first item the team developed was in response to complaints from many women that their makeup stayed on after they'd used a cleanser. They created Erika Cleanser, which "cleans the skin while removing makeup at the same time."

A strong believer in what she calls "pure natural things," Wilkins finds "many women feel they have to put on a lot of makeup to look beautiful, but I disagree. Erika products are created to bring out the inner qualities that are already there. We carry formulated makeup that will enhance black women's skin tones. Making women look beautiful is what I'm good at. I'm so proud to generate in other women a desire to look their best," Wilkins notes.

The sixty sales reps for Erika Cosmetics have all come by referral and word of mouth, in Texas, Florida, New York, and New Jersey. Erica Wilkins recruits women seeking "something other than a nine-to-five job, who always wanted to be part of the beauty industry." Wilkins founded her company as "the first black-owned natural cosmetics firm." A representative's $175 investment buys a kit of product samples and several individual training sessions. "We teach our reps how to get referrals and keep records. Meetings every three weeks provide further training, motivation, and marketing strategy," Wilkins reports.

Its line of natural products, specially formulated for black women, includes nail polish, lipstick, lip pencil, lip glaze, eye shadow, eye pencil, pressed powder, cover-up, mousse, liquid makeup, mascara, and a skin care line (moisturizer, cleanser, toner, mask, etc.) "Black companies have never emphasized black skin care. We want women to understand and value good skin care. Erika's purpose is to bring the best products to our customers, offering them clean, healthy skin and a better understanding of how they can look truly beautiful," says the president of the company.

Crafts Dealer

Cathy Comins was president of the Montclair Crafters' Guild (New Jersey) when she started selling "handcrafted rugs for floors and walls. I work on consignment and ask the artists to do special themes for particular events," says Comins, who "lugs rugs" from her home office. Customers find her at charity exhibitions (where she may have donated a rug), in textile courses, or through ads in industry publications and directories. Art Underfoot also sends mailings and makes cold calls to interior designers. With artists and clients all over the country, Comins is pleased her rugs have been seen in *House & Garden.*

Having headed the ninety-member Crafters' Guild for over six years, Comins also runs the Montclair Crafts Show as a volunteer. It draws 3,500 attendees. Her paid job, selling advertising space for a national publication, was profitable but boring. "I was eager for creativity," remembers Comins. "When I saw someone making a traditionally hooked rug, with woolen fabric, not yarn, I was mesmerized by the process." She'd always been interested in crafts, and Comins's research showed that antique hooked rugs were available, but new ones were hard to find. "I searched for and discovered many hookers around America who would part with rugs for customers." Her information sources included crafts stores and crafts writers. She got the first rugs on consignment.

"First I found the stockpilers, then the people who were in it to sell. Through the business, I've also found weavers and braiders, so I can offer custom room-sized rugs." Her biggest start-up cost was a computer; the only other equipment needed was a telephone. With artists and designers all over the country, Comins carries custom-made, hard-to-find rag or braid rugs.

Initially she worked with slides, but now has a Polaroid camera so she can photograph items she's selling. The business still operates out of her home; insurance protects the rugs. An attorney drafted what Comins calls her "fancy contracts." Her biggest problem? "Finding the market has been the hardest part," Cathy Comins admits.

Dressmaker

Laura James spends forty hours a week on her "part-time" dressmaking business, La-Privajj, which began in Panama many years ago. James, who came to the United States over a decade ago, makes scarves, hats, bridal outfits, and even bags, in addition to clothing. She does custom-design work and alterations from her home sewing room, where she works evenings and weekends, and gets occasional help from family members. By day, she's a sales rep for a cosmetics company.

James has never done any paid promotion for La-Privajj. "My clothes that I wear are my best advertisement. People ask where I got them, and become clients." James also gets customers by word of mouth and referrals from the Black Fashion Museum, where she's a member of the board. She's Corresponding Secretary of the National Association of Milliners, Tailors, and Dressmakers. Her copy of Mary Todd Lincoln's inaugural dress was exhibited at the Black Fashion Museum, and several of her gowns were used by *Bride's* magazine for a photo shoot.

Event Planner

Many years ago, Donna Friedman was an executive secretary at an insurance company, a part-time M.B.A. student, and Grape Jelly the Clown on weekends. A corporate executive who had admired Grape Jelly's work at company parties hired Friedman to plan the grand-opening celebration for Merrill Lynch's new headquarters, and her home-based event planning firm was born. "I had four weeks to put that entire event together," Friedman remembers in amazement.

Performing at a company picnic as Grape Jelly, she impressed a department store executive, who recommended her to colleagues. Friedman followed up by sending a letter of introduction to the store's vice president. On the strength of the letter, the executive suggested her to several branch managers. Soon Friedman was getting calls from some of the fourteen branches to coordinate events. Because she still had her full-time job at the insurance company, Friedman held auditions to find her performers at 7:30 A.M., at lunchtime, and in the evenings. She went on attending night classes for her M.B.A. (at least for a while).

For Christmas that year, she had fourteen actors in fourteen stores over a ten-day period. They presented breakfast with Santa programs, magic shows, and twenty-five Santa imitators on a throne. A month later, Friedman's employer moved to another state, and Exceptional Entertainment became her full-time business.

The company arranges parties, picnics, and special events for corporations. It will write and stage a play or any kind of performance a client wants. "For large enough occasions, we also do private parties, including weddings," notes Friedman, but their main market is corporate. Exceptional Entertainment gets clients through its ads in special-event magazines, booths at trade shows, and networking at business organizations like the local chamber of commerce. Word of mouth has been helpful, too.

Friedman's own background, apart from clowning, included singing and acting. She feels her business skills have been extremely valuable, as was the fact that she had a personal computer at home when she started the company. "It was so handy for late-night work at the beginning," she observes. Today, the company has a full-time secretary and four coordinators, plus a stable of writers, directors, florists and caterers on call. Exceptional Entertainment's clients include Citibank, Benetton, Schlumberger, and Filene's. "You have to be creative, organized, flexible, and thorough, with a sense of humor," says Friedman. "My trade secret is knowing where to find exceptional performers."

Gardener

To subsidize her salary as director and curator of a small suburban museum, Evelyn Tully Costa put fliers on the security system gates of Eastern Long Island mansions to offer estate-sitting services. "An Italian count with an ailing rose garden called. I bought a book, studied hard, and restored his roses," Costa recalls. Returning to her city residence several years ago, she saw gardens all around. So Costa advertised in local papers and kept studying. Today, Garden Services has "more business than I know what to do with," reveals its owner.

Traveling by bike, with her hand clippers, pruners, and trowel, Costa designs and plants patios, gardens, and Xeriscapes (arrangements of drought-resistant flowers and shrubs requiring no water) for urban dwellers. Not having a truck proved to be easily resolved: most nurseries deliver. She often orders plants by mail and has construction materials brought to the client's home. "If I can't get there in fifteen minutes, I don't go," says Costa, whose only start-up cost was her gardening tools. Busy eight months a year, she sees two clients a day, usually working with the same garden three or four times a year. Concerned about both recycling and community service, Costa donates her excess dirt, trees, and shrubs to the Green Guerrillas, an environmental group. She's vehemently opposed to pesticides and never uses them, claiming, "Ladybugs kill aphids," and employing holistic approaches. She encourages clients to subscribe to *Organic Gardening*. Often working along with a client, Costa may be hired to redo an entire yard.

In her staff position, Costa missed being out in the open. She now takes six weeks off in summer and two or three months in winter. Spring and fall are busy, with planting and cleanup. Costa does not work in the rain or when the temperature falls below thirty-two degrees. She has a four-hour minimum. "I love to garden," avers Evelyn Tully Costa. "I take care of everyone's plants like they're my own."

Image Consultant

An initial investment of under $1,000 bought Raven A. Wilson all her equipment and specialized training at Beauty for All Seasons (Idaho) and Image Reflections International. "I contacted friends and family to tell them about my business, then got referrals," reports the image consultant, who advertised First Impressions in a local monthly newspaper and spread the word at professional associations. Wilson's firm provides figure and style analysis, wardrobe planning, closet audits, skin care, and color analysis. She will select cosmetics and show a client how to apply makeup.

Men as well as women have sought Wilson's services. She gives talks to groups in her city, like the Rotary club, and has been hired by the Bulova Watch School and other career training institutes to advise their students who will soon be job-hunting. She presents her scarf-tying workshop at popular local boutiques, and draws students to her Saturday exercise class. During the week, Wilson works at a public school until 3:00 P.M., which leaves ample late afternoon and evening hours for First Impressions. She also appreciates having time available to spend with her son.

Wilson used a beautiful burgundy and gray business card and promoted her business with attractive fliers, in addition to ads and networking. After six years in operation, she felt it was time for a brochure and hired my firm to prepare one. It matches her business card, features a photo of the company founder, and is receiving positive response.

Personal Shopper

Personal shopper Tracy Kendall buys clothes, gifts, accessories, and shoes for other people. "Some clients come along on the shopping trips; others just tell me what they want," explains Kendall, who services both individuals and advertising agencies.

"I'm a priest of clothing. A lot of people shop in pieces and don't know how to put things together. You have to be tactful in telling someone this is wrong for their type." Other requirements are good taste and keen listening skills. "You have to be decisive, a quick study with a sixth sense, and have an instinct about how much a client will accept change."

An underlying need Kendall discovered is simple hand-holding. Her main expense is classified advertising in her city's weekly magazine and in a weekly community newspaper, and periodic direct-mail promotions. She charges $50 an hour, with a two-hour minimum, and hopes clients will begin to hire her to purchase home furnishings.

"This is a very personal service, and my ads seem to bring a lot of people out of the woodwork," reports Kendall, who is having a great deal of fun shopping for others.

Pet- and Plant-Sitter

"For ten years, I'd been cat- and plant-sitting for friends and neighbors," says Toni Bettis, a former children's wear designer. "After my daughter was born, I couldn't continue my freelance design work, so I decided to try a career the baby wouldn't distract me from. Since I love animals, I had cards and fliers made up for While You're Away."

In her new enterprise, for which she is bonded, Bettis walks dogs, changes kitty litter, feeds and brushes pets, waters plants, and forwards mail for absent owners. Visits average thirty minutes. "After you get customers who like you, you get repeat business. Advertising has been my big expense," notes Bettis, who obtains good results from her classified ad in a weekly magazine and popular neighborhood news-papers, which are distributed for free.

Promotional Items Dealer

Sarah Taub got her first customers several years ago by leaving pens, pencils, and magnetic clip holders imprinted with her company name. Since Advance Specialties sells promotional items, the samples showed prospects how effective they can be.

"A friend who happened to be an experienced novelty item distri-butor gave me leads about sources of merchandise and prospects," Taub recalls. Her friend stressed the value of approaching newer companies in the process of developing a client base. Taking his advice, she began telephoning new businesses in her neighborhood and suggesting to the owners "that they could benefit from promotional items to get their names known. Older businesses already had sources for these kinds of items, but for new companies, imprinted promotional merchandise can really help."

Taub never advertised for her first two years, getting all her clients by cold calls. She pays for merchandise only as ordered; her suppliers provide catalogs and "sell sheets" (a page of information, usually illustrated with the product) for the items they will imprint for her customers.

Public Relations

When she left her job heading a university's communications department, Renee Sacks, then a single mother, had a small consulting practice translating legal documents into plain language and helping real estate firms with their marketing needs. From her basement in a waterfront community twenty miles from the main business district of her city, Sacks's persistence and personal referrals helped her generate her first two accounts.

For the next two years, she bartered corporate communications services in exchange for space in a downtown office. "Our first bartered space was a cubbyhole, so I moved up to five hundred square feet at another company. Reciprocity is one way for a young company with a good idea to grow," Sacks believes. As business increased, she began hiring employees and soon outgrew the second office.

In its fourth year, Renee Sacks Associates moved to five thousand square feet in the heart of the business district. Today, seventeen employees serve law firms, Realtors, and professional associations, which find Renee Sacks Associates through referrals or through seminars that the public relations firm presents. "Most of our work is business to business, and we do a lot of networking," says Sacks. "Running those public programs keeps our name visible. Almost every time we put on a seminar, I get a client." The firm grossed $1 million the year it moved to larger quarters.

Résumé Service

Marge Gronski started Career Advantage, her résumé service, by putting fliers in nearby stationery stores and placing ads in local papers. Her first customers were soon referring friends and fellow students. Career Advantage will organize the information for a client's résumé, recommend the best wording, devise an attractive layout, and produce either a single original suitable for reproducing or a small number of copies the client may need, printed out on appropriate paper.

Gronski paid for advice from some consultants and took the basic course at American Women's Economic Development Corporation. She hired a very professional-sounding answering service to give callers the impression she has a larger staff. "To keep start-up costs down, rent or lease a good word processor and printer," she suggests. "Learning by doing, and making mistakes, is the absolute best teacher."

Secretarial Service

Joanie Colaluca launched Home Touch, her "private secretarial service," by mailing a simple flier and business card to names she chose from the phone book in her affluent suburban town. She hired my firm to create the mailer, her only start-up expense.

"On October 21, I mailed the first twenty fliers—and my first response was on October 23!" Colaluca reported excitedly. She began working with her initial client, a famous entertainer, in November. At customers' homes or offices, Colaluca takes dictation, handles correspondence, balances checkbooks, makes phone calls, pays bills, handwrites invitations, etc.

Word and Data Processing

After twenty years of office experience, Kathleen Burke invested $1,300 in a personal computer and printer. She then opened her new word- and data-processing service in her home. When she met with me for marketing assistance, I suggested the name she later adopted: Burke's Bytes.

After reading about the service in local ads and fliers, clients started bringing résumés, play scripts, mailing lists, proposals, and reports to the firm. Burke can read, write, and edit in Spanish, German, French, and Russian. She also has computer software in Greek and Russian. "Burke's Bytes translates correspondence and handles bookkeeping for small businesses," says Burke, who registered her company name but elected to save money by not installing a separate business phone. She's been surprised and gratified by the array of projects clients have brought to her in her early years of operation.

The next two chapters will outline an array of inexpensive marketing methods, including some of the approaches these women used to get started on very limited capital.

10

Secrets of Low-Cost Marketing

*B*efore you open for business, you have to plan the ways in which you'll attract customers. Marketing does not require a lavish budget, but it does call for persistence, ingenuity, determination, or sales ability. In this chapter, a variety of methods chosen by other shoestring entrepreneurs to lure their early clients will be highlighted.

But first, an important definition. To me, marketing means: identify a need and show how you are uniquely qualified to meet it.

The trick to keeping your marketing costs low is to know exactly who your target customers are (which you've already figured out in chapter 8) and then determine the least expensive ways to let them know about your services.

The fundamental task in marketing is to pinpoint the need you are meeting. Exactly what problem do you solve? You distilled your service and your U.S.P. into a twenty-five-word sentence. The next step is to focus on why someone should hire or buy from you.

Milano's First Rule of Marketing: If it doesn't take a lot of money, it costs you time. Of which do you have more? The answer will vary at different points in your professional life, but for many new business owners, it's time.

Milano's Second Rule: Everything you do to promote your business has to match the image you're trying to establish. Once you've decided how you want the public to perceive you, be consistent in the way you present yourself and your product or service.

The following suggestions are my twenty-seven favorite low-cost marketing techniques.

Try Fliers

A very inexpensive method, fliers are effective for any business offering something many consumers need. Kathleen Lewis, who founded Pinch Sitters, mailed fliers to all the local nursery schools and day-care centers to hang on their bulletin boards, which gave her new firm immediate credibility. Merry Marks launched Dustbusters, her cleaning company, by putting five hundred fliers on neighborhood cars each weekend. Like Marks, a photographer who specializes in portraits of children and families introduced his storefront studio in my community by putting fliers on local automobiles. As long as your fliers support the image you want to maintain, you can hang them yourself, at supermarkets, banks, and on community bulletin boards. Even a flier distribution service, which will put them in residential mailboxes or under household doors, is moderately priced.

Be Visible in Your Community

Another way to reach consumers is to take a booth at community fairs and street festivals, where you can give away samples or demonstrate what you do. Donate prizes in raffles or contests, making sure to get a noticeable credit line for each item you contribute. Sponsor a local event, like a house tour, concert, or wine tasting to benefit a nonprofit organization. In return, the organization will feature your sponsorship in all its publicity, and your business will develop some positive visibility.

Advertise

Any kind of advertising must be repeated to have an impact. Seeing your name regularly will eventually teach buyers what you offer as well as build a feeling that you're reliable. Help people in your area learn about your competitive prices, high quality, and attentive service by advertising in community weekly publications, often distributed free to residents. My desktop publisher, George Fiala, tests his new ads in the low-cost classified section of community newspapers. "Be sure to track your advertising," he advises. "Ask each caller where he or she heard of you. When you see which publication works best, switch to a display ad in that paper and cut back on your other advertising."

Use the Yellow Pages

With a business phone number, you receive a free listing in the local Yellow Pages. In addition, many businesses place a display ad in the Yellow Pages, requiring an annual contract for which you'll be billed in twelve monthly installments (on each phone bill). You'll have an entire year to see if the ad brings the kind of callers who become customers. By the way, since phone book readers tend to look down the column, firms at the beginning of the alphabet get the largest number of inquiries. An inquiry is not a sale, though. If you find you're getting too many calls from people looking for something you do not offer, this means you're wasting a lot of your time. You may want to consider shifting to a different category for the following year's edition.

Try Trade Publications

If you're offering a service to other businesses, track the trade papers your prospects are likely to read. Classified ads in trade publications are surprisingly inexpensive and destined to be seen by the precise audience you want to reach. You can also advertise in the newsletters of professional associations whose members are likely to need your services; these are also very low cost. (Unfortunately, some association newsletters do not accept advertising.)

Offer Free Information

Giving away information that's valuable to your prospects will get them to think of you. A few years ago, my firm helped launch a new elevator consulting company. Adapting charts and forms used by the founder in his work, I created an inexpensive fourteen-page booklet that we named "Owner's Guide to Better Elevator Service." I sent a brief press release announcing the free handbook to every trade publication in the consultant's target markets; most printed it. The owner stacked handbooks at his trade show booths, gave them out at his talks, and mailed them to anyone who called in response to the free publicity. I ghostwrote articles for him when trade press editors asked if he'd contribute something. The handbook/publicity blitz brought the elevator consulting firm several impressive real estate and commercial clients and got his business off the ground.

Check Out Trade Shows

Attending exhibitions in your own field tells you what's going on, which is important. To generate some business, you can visit a trade show where your clients display their wares. It's wise to do a little research in advance. Graphic designer Jewel Feldman wanted more assignments creating writing papers. At the National Stationery Show, she studied the list of exhibitors before going inside the convention center. On the floor plan, she located the booths of some companies whose lines she felt matched her style. Carrying a small portfolio of her work, she engaged company salespeople in conversation, got the names of the right people to contact at each company, and soon landed two freelance assignments.

Give Valuable Advice

Show a potential customer how he or she can save money. An enterprising printing broker secured a major health-club chain as her account after she examined an odd-sized postcard it sent her. She called a club executive to say, "Did you know you could save a fortune in postage if you made this card just one-quarter inch smaller on each side? No one would notice and it wouldn't change the design at all." Impressed with her cost-conscious perspective, the owner invited her in for a meeting, and she began handling all the company's printing shortly afterward.

Keep On Calling

Telephone tenacity can really pay off. When illustrator Dana Schreiber relocated to New England, he joined the Connecticut Art Directors Club. Compiling a mailing list from its membership directory, he called every ad agency to verify names and addresses for each person on his list because people change jobs so often. After the mailing, Schreiber made follow-up phone calls to request interviews, showed his work, and kept calling back—for nearly a year—at the largest advertising agency in Hartford. Frustrated, he finally phoned the production manager to say, "I've worked for everyone else in this area—except you." His persistence won him a small assignment, during which the artist made sure to meet agency art directors. Gradually, he began getting better projects from the big agency.

Build a Referral Network

Seek out people who can refer customers to you. Look for professionals in adjacent fields and go introduce yourself. For example, as a marketing writer, I make a point of contacting graphic designers, desktop publishers, and production firms with clients similar to mine. Both my printer and my computer graphics specialist have referred clients to me. Establishing a mutual referral arrangement is very worthwhile.

Try Inexpensive Direct Mail

Postcards are an effective way to catch attention. My company creates big black-and-white postcards with a single-panel cartoon spoofing the problem a client solves for other businesses. Response is always good because the front of the card elicits a smile and shows a firm grasp of the prospect's need. People keep the postcards in drawers or on bulletin boards until they require the service that's shown. (I finally teamed up with my cartoonist and my mailing house to design a postcard promoting our services and was immediately hired by someone I'd known for years!)

Seek Out Your Customers

Go where your prospects are. You found out what they read and to which associations they belong. Now track down the meeting times and places of those professional groups and see if you can attend meetings as a guest (or join as an associate member). Make sure people you meet at these gatherings know what you do and that you specialize in providing services to their industry. Always follow up with either a request for a get-together, or, at the very least, a note with a sample of your work or additional information about your service. The more often people see you at their professional meetings, the more they will come to think of you as someone who is connected to their field. (Add to that perception by scanning their trade papers regularly so you know the major concerns of the industry.)

Write a Letter

Send a forceful sales letter. A graphic designer asked me to write a letter he could send to small- or medium-sized public relations firms in his city. By studying his portfolio, I identified his U.S.P. and crafted a one-page letter explaining just how he could meet the specific needs that a public relations agency is likely to have. A sample sheet showing his work accompanied the letter, printed on his studio's beautiful letterhead. From a current directory of public relations firms, the designer had identified one hundred that fit the profile he found most promising. I recommended he mail twenty letters a week, so he'd have time for follow-up calls to each. The designer got a stunning 25 percent response: when he phoned the public relations firms, one out of every four executives invited him to come in with his portfolio!

Use Your Telephone

Targeted telemarketing—yes, the cold call—can be a labor-intensive but inexpensive business builder. Telemarketing works best when it is carefully planned. At one of my lectures, a C.P.A. in private practice shared his successful promotion technique. Having pinpointed his target customer as a business too small for a full-time accounting staff, he compiles a prospect list by collecting ads and little items about small companies from local newspapers. On his calendar every week, the accountant blocks out a full day or two half days to make phone calls on this list. He makes sixty to seventy-five cold calls per day. When he doesn't reach the owner, he leaves a mysterious message: name, phone number, "please call." His theory that entrepreneurs always return calls from anyone who might be a potential customer is more than valid. Tracking the costs and results of his telemarketing campaign, he finds it brings him many new clients.

Help People Dial Your Number

You can help people remember your firm by arranging for an alpha phone number, which allows callers simply to dial a word. A company in my city got off to a great start by inviting the public to dial 800-FLOWERS when they wanted to arrange delivery of a bouquet. To find out if the word you would like to use for your business number is already in use in your area, dial it and see who answers. If it's another business, you'll have to try a different catchword. If it's a residence, though, the local phone company can often work out an arrangement with the home that has the number you'd like to use. Alpha numbers are not more expensive, and what a great aid to customers!

Place Your Literature Strategically

As you gain a surer sense of your audience, put your literature where your prospects can see it. Try to stack your brochures or promotion pieces where your clients are likely to pass by. For a real consumer-oriented service, many businesses utilize supermarket entryways or twenty-four-hour bank machine cubicles. Some public libraries allow providers of services relevant to library patrons to leave their material. A word-processing, tutoring, or editing business, whose customers often include students, would be appropriate. For business-to-business offerings, consider photocopy or fax shops, or local small printers. Assuming you're a customer, ask permission to put some small promotion pieces in a corner or on a shelf. If this makes the owner uncomfortable, see if you can at least hang a small ad on the bulletin board.

Exhibit at a Trade Show

Both Erica Gjersvik of Pangaea and Samone Jaspers of Fiore built their fledgling firms by investing in a booth at the right trade show. While this will take a sizable bite out of your $2,000 budget, it will give you priceless exposure to the very buyers you must meet to get your business off the ground. You'll need to invest time in follow-up calls to and meetings with buyers who stop at your booth.

Turn to Unusual Sources

You can even prospect for clients in the daily newspaper. When Susan Winer, president of Stratenomics, started out, she was convinced that just because her Chicago strategic planning firm was small, it didn't have to pursue little accounts. Aiming at mid- to large-sized corporations within 150 miles, Winer explains, "We went through the Sunday *Chicago Tribune* classified section looking for companies with new positions to fill. We'd call up, get the name of the person in charge of the expanding department, and send a letter offering Stratenomics's expertise in the area" (on a consulting basis). Turning any possible negative into an asset, Winer carefully positioned her firm as innovative and experienced, rather than small or new. She's convinced it's her assertive approach that has always landed Stratenomics large, well-known corporations as clients.

Gather Some Contacts Together

Are you going out on your own in a field in which you know quite a few people? You might adopt a technique that works for Pro-Action Training Company, which presents communications workshops for Fortune 500 companies. "My big secret of success is breakfast," confides Barbara Sacker, the president. Carefully maintaining contacts she's made throughout her career, Sacker invites six people who don't know each other to her monthly networking breakfasts at elegant downtown restaurants, ending up with three or four (including herself). "You miss the conversation with more," notes Sacker, who chose the morning meal to contain costs. "Even with four people, breakfast for four at a lovely restaurant is about $60." Guests are previous clients or former business acquaintances. Though no selling goes on at the breakfasts, "Lots of business growth has resulted," Sacker admits.

Knock on Doors

Even today, door-to-door selling can work. One of my clients nearly hired an accountant who unexpectedly knocked on her office door just as she was contemplating a change in accounting firms. She interviewed and seriously considered the visitor's proposal. This is both a time-consuming and -honored method of soliciting new business. If you have the hours, the stamina, and the temperament for it, the door-to-door route is worth considering.

Show Off Your Expertise

Once you declare your area of expertise, two kinds of exposure can enhance your credibility and your sales. See if you can write a column for a publication that reaches your target audience. Offer to donate it to any suitable weekly or monthly community or trade newspaper. You'll be instantly viewed as an expert in your field. When people see your ads or fliers after they've read your column, the impact is enhanced. After joining the local chamber of commerce, I badgered the public relations director to let me contribute a column to its monthly newspaper. Two clients hired me because they saw my column. (Do not use modest writing skills as an excuse! For a very nominal fee, you can hire a journalism student at the nearest college to craft a column for you. Famous authorities frequently have ghostwriters polish their prose— so can you.)

In addition to the column, you can give a talk or demonstration about your specialty to an appropriate group. If you own a renovation company, offer to talk to a large condominium association about affordable remodeling approaches. An image consultant can speak to any professional association about the best ways to make a striking first impression. This chapter is adapted from "Secrets of Low-Cost Marketing," a speech I often give to business groups. A big advantage of giving a talk is the "multiplier effect": not only do fifty or one hundred people learn about your services, but many of them may mention you later on to some of the hundreds of people they know. So be sure to bring along something with your name and phone number for audience members to take to remember you by!

(A word of caution: while you can easily hire a ghostwriter to work wonders on your writing, don't choose public speaking until you've had some practice at it. Because this is such a useful knack, you may want to seek out the nearest branch of Toastmasters, an international organization that helps its members to develop their public speaking skills, or sign up for a public speaking course at a Dale Carnegie facility.)

More Advanced Techniques

The longer you're in business, the more promotional paths you'll be able to pursue. Here are four possibilities to consider when you've been dealing with your customers for more than six months and know more about their concerns.

Try a Cross-Promotion

Team up with another business seeking the same kinds of customers you are, and do a joint mailing or ad campaign. A dry cleaner and a restaurant in my neighborhood did an interesting cross-promotion. At Ralph's Cleaners, customers could pick up a card offering them $5 off on their next meal at Aunt Suzie's. At the restaurant, patrons received a coupon for 20 percent off their next dry-cleaning bill at Ralph's. My desktop publisher cross-promotes with a nearby copy shop. At each site, cards touting the other service are prominently displayed on the counter.

Organize a Panel

Once you've identified other (unrelated) businesses seeking your kind of customer, you can arrange a panel or seminar with several of them. For example, if you run a baby-sitting service and can talk about some child-care issues, invite a financial planner to discuss saving for college tuition, a travel agent who specializes in family vacations, and a pediatrician or child psychologist to join a panel at a local nursery school. Give the evening or weekend forum a catchy name (perhaps "Raising a Child in a Two-Career Family"), send announcements to all the local newspapers, and post brightly colored fliers where parents are sure to see them. At the panel, leave ample time for questions and answers, and tell all the participants to bring a lot of literature. (Again, it's hard to join a panel if you're not used to public speaking. I'm rerecommending Toastmasters.)

Provide News to Your Prospects

Send a newsletter containing some helpful material, so your clients and prospects will hang on to it. This is a subtle sales tool, since it shows how involved you are in your field and how much you know about it. Newsletters do not have to be expensive, but they do have to maintain your image and communicate something that can be vaguely classified as "news." Many of the newsletters I do for small businesses contain an update on the firm's activities, some kind of how-to article that's useful to the reader, a little section of tips, and perhaps an interview with someone to whom readers can relate. It's a good opportunity to let people know about new equipment, a new technique, or a new employee in your office. In many industries, like health care, you can order well-produced newsletters from national companies that create them. Your company name will be imprinted on each copy, so a reader assumes your firm created them. This is a very convenient approach; the only negative is that none of the material will throw a spotlight on anything your own company is doing. For comparison, check with a desktop publisher about the costs of creating your own newsletter.

This is the final secret about marketing: spend your time on the things you do well. Creating powerful promotional material is a very particular skill. For cost-effective promotion, maximize your marketing money by getting expert help. You may think it costs more to hire an expert to help you, but marketing is one area where you can throw out a lot of money very quickly if you haven't planned carefully (see chapter 12 for tips on developing your marketing plan).

The Internet

Since the publication of the first edition of *Hers* in 1991, the Internet has become a valuable means of national and international communication—and marketing. The Internet not only allows you to advertise your existence to millions, via a Web page, but, unlike magazine or newspaper ads, it also allows customers to respond immediately, via e-mail, making it "interactive" advertising. Already, millions of potential consumers have Internet access in North America. If your service or product might flourish with that kind of exposure, read the next chapter!

∼

11

What About
a Web Site?

*G*iven the surging popularity and success of the Internet as a marketing tool, the revised edition of *Hers* would be incomplete without some mention of it. Although many polls indicate that most Internet users are men, a recent survey by the National Foundation for Women Business Owners shows that woman business owners are equally cognizant of the potential of the Net and the World Wide Web.

The following chapter was excerpted and slightly adapted from *The Internet Publicity Guide: How to Maximize Your Marketing and Promotion in Cyberspace* by V. A. Shiva (New York: Allworth Press, 1997). Besides explaining how your business can take advantage of the Internet's promotional potential, Shiva's book provides information about Web page design and clear definitions of Netsurfing terminology.

What Is a Web Site?

For starters, consider a Web site as the electronic version of your current print brochures or materials. In traditional materials, you use graphics, text, and design elements to represent yourself or your company in the best way. A Web site contains similar information, which has been digitized and laid out in a format for viewing on a computer screen. All your material is accessible to anyone who has your Web site address on the Internet.

Why Create a Web Site?

The reason to create a Web site is the array of opportunities it affords. A successful Web site can:

- generate valuable leads and mailing lists of prospective clients
- create awareness of your products and services among an audience you may never have reached otherwise
- provide detailed presales information on you and your organization
- increase your profits by attracting new customers from the World Wide Web's 20 million young, educated professionals with household incomes above $50,000
- create new sales channels you won't find anywhere else
- distribute your products faster and more flexibly
- position your company strategically for the twenty-first century
- improve customer service
- enable you to update your information instantaneously and often
- collect prospective client demographics
- find new partners and allies around the world

The cost of creating a Web site and making your Web site address accessible to the many millions of people on the Web is pennies compared to traditional means of advertising and communication. That's why people say the Web "levels the playing field." A local recording artist in Arkansas has equal access to a Web site as a major multibillion-dollar corporation. However, that same local artist, unlikely to win a guest spot on a major television program, can reach a bigger audience on the Web.

The Basics

A Web site is only as good as the number and kind of people who come to it. Once you have spent a great deal of time getting on the Internet and building your Web site, you cannot afford to neglect cyberpublicity: the art and science of promoting your presence in cyberspace and getting the kind of exposure you need. Cyberpublicity will also serve to give you statistics on the number of people who visit your site, so you'll gain useful demographic information on your electronic prospects.

Who Am I?

The first step in cyberpublicity is to determine who you are. You should take some time to think about it. I normally recommend that clients take paper and pen, or word processor and keyboard, and jot down words or phrases that describe them. Most people (or business owners) know who they are but have never tried to categorize themselves in words and concepts. The end product of this exercise should be one paragraph, at most fifty words, describing who you are; up to twenty keywords that characterize your organization; up to ten words that describe the broad categories related to your organization.

Recently, I helped to cyberpublicize a small-business owner who owns and operates an independent record label. She wrote a fifty-word statement describing the business, the mission of the label, and the kinds of musicians it services. Next, she gave me the following keywords: *new age, music, soft, easy listening, contemporary, New York, haunting, award-winning, Celtic, musician, guitar, flute, vocal, piano, sitar, Indian, bamboo,* and *Grammy.* These keywords reflected the traits of the organization. Finally, she gave me a list of ten words describing the categories under which the organization could be indexed: *weddings, concerts, labels, distributors, retailer, music, awards, entertainment, Celtic,* and *Indian.*

This type of information is central to starting a cyberpublicity campaign. Take time to get the keywords and categories right before proceeding.

Netiquette

Once you have taken the time to figure out who you are, you are ready to start your cyberpublicity campaign. But before taking any direct action, you need to understand the nature of your medium and the rules of the game. Users of the Internet, including the Web and UseNet, are expected to follow a set of guidelines for their behavior, called *netiquette.* The complete guide to netiquette is available through another newsgroup called *news.announce.newusers,* which has articles on the latest guidelines. Before you begin to communicate your information using e-mail, newsgroups, or the Web, I encourage you to read the articles at that newsgroup thoroughly.

One netiquette rule is that insulting, degrading, or racist comments are intolerable, unless you are in one of the underground "alt" newsgroups. It is also important to keep your communications succinct. If you are excerpting or quoting someone else's article in your communication, keep the excerpt short and relevant to your communication. Despite what newspapers and some public relations companies say, newsgroups are really not for promoting business items, advertisements, get-rich-quick schemes, or other similar postings. Blatant postings to solicit customers are unequivocally condemned. It is acceptable, however, to mention a service, Web site, local store, or company, in the context of the rest of the articles posted in a newsgroup. Direct soliciting is considered forbidden. Multilevel marketing schemes, form letters, and other such methods are a major breach of netiquette. While the users of the Internet may not have direct control of what you communicate, the Internet is very quick to condemn that kind of behavior.

Cross Links

Linking your Web site to other related sites and directories is the first step in your cyberpublicity campaign. The ten words you chose earlier to describe your Web site helps identify those Web directories and indexes to which your site should be linked. Post your site address to as many relevant directories and indexes as possible. I always encourage clients to post their Web site address to the top five Web search engines: Yahoo, WebCrawler, Lycos, InfoSeek, and Excite. It costs you nothing to post on these directories.

Surf the Internet to find other Web sites similar to yours. Many other sites can serve as perfect jump sites to your own. Once you find a site that attracts a similar audience to yours, find the e-mail account of the Webmaster, or the person in charge of running the Web site. Send an e-mail to this person asking for a reciprocal hyperlink. Explain that you will provide a hyperlink to his or her site, if he or she provides one to yours. This is a great way to become known within your audience, by narrowcasting on the Internet. Posting your Web site at popular sites similar to yours can make your location an overnight success.

Newsgroups

The next major area for posting your Web site address is UseNet newsgroups on the Internet. These very specific groups are easy to subscribe to and post messages on. A discussion group exists for almost any topic imaginable. By analyzing the words and categories you use to describe yourself, you should be able to find relevant newsgroups. Newsgroups may reach hundreds of thousands of users every day, so make sure your postings are well thought out.

Experiment with newsgroups and you will notice the most effective postings are well reasoned, logical, and properly laid out, with good grammar and spelling. They don't ramble. Adopt this pattern. Remember, some users come to the Internet via some other online service, such as America Online or Microsoft Network, and pay by the hour to receive their newsgroup information. Nothing will annoy them more than paying for long and pointless postings. Keep this in mind when you write. Some subjects need many lines of explanation, but do not use up valuable space to say nothing.

Good grammar and spelling are sometimes difficult to maintain when typing quickly, but do try. Your presentation reflects the image and credibility you worked hard to create. Construct sentences properly.

An odd spelling mistake is easily tolerated; a series of them invites disdain. Make sure you post informative messages to the group. Any message directly promoting your Web site is considered improper netiquette.

In terms of netiquette, the best method of promoting your Web site is to participate in an ongoing newsgroup discussion. At the bottom of each article you post, make sure your signature has your Web site address. A signature is a several-line block of text that can be added to any article that you post on a newsgroup. Using signatures is an accepted form of advertisement that can bring many people to your site. Do not just join a newsgroup and leave a message like, "Hi! My name is _____, come visit my Web site at _____." You will suffer the wrath of that newsgroup. Become an active participant in the group's discussion and offer information to the newsgroup. Find ways to mention your Web site in the context of the newsgroup's discussion. You will get what you give. This kind of interaction takes more time than simply posting your Web site address on a directory or search engine, but is well worth it.

Cross-Publicize

We still live in a physical world, so market your Web site address also using traditional methods. Publicity should not exist in a vacuum; cyberpublicity is no exception. If you spend money to set up your online presence, protect that investment by promoting your online Web site address in brochures, at performances, shows, in press releases, etc. Use your new Web site address in your advertising and on your business cards.

Mention your Web site address in radio spots and magazines or newspaper ads. If you do it right, you will add value to your traditional publicity by enabling people to go to cyberspace to get more information about you. Such cross-publicity increases the value of your traditional advertising; it would cost a fortune to include all the information on your Web site in print, TV, or radio ads. Promoting your

Web site address on traditional publicity materials offers a physical hyperlink to your cyberspace billboard.

Hold Promotional Offers

Put promotional offers on your site. Offer discounts on products or tickets for customers who visit your Web site. Promotional offers are a way to continue the cycle of cyberpublicity on a regular basis. It is not sufficient to cyberpublicize only once. Creating promotional offers or new features gives a reason to continue the cycle of cyberpublicity.

Guest Book and E-Mail

Internet publicity is based on feedback from your audience—a key difference from traditional publicity. Guest book and e-mail forwarding are two vehicles for transmitting feedback.

A guest book can be a simple form containing fields such as name, address, phone, e-mail address, and zip code that you ask Web site visitors to fill out when they visit your site. Most visitors will not fill out such a form unless you either offer them something (a promotion) or ask them a question that requires their input. You need to be clever and creative to get people to fill out your guest book. You could, for example, give a visitor 5 to 10 percent off the price of tickets, CDs, purchases, etc., for filling out the guest book. Their entries become a valuable resource and a mailing list of future clients.

Adding an e-mail forwarding link to your Web site is a must. An e-mail forwarding link will allow visitors to contact you directly. Visitors can give their comments on your Web site, as well as feedback on the service or product you provide.

Acquiring Demographics

Unlike traditional publicity and advertising, the Internet lets you know, numerically, how effective your publicity efforts are. The Internet maintains log files, which can be used to determine the number of unique visitors coming to your site. Each entry is stamped with the date, time, and address of a remote visitor. One frequent mistake is to count each entry in the log file as a unique visitor to the Web site. Each entry records everything from the user accessing text to images; therefore, a single user requesting a single document might actually result in several entries in the log file as the document and related images are being received.

Suppose you run an art gallery on the Web. You may have done all your cyberpublicity on Web directories, newsgroups, etc., and are now interested in knowing how many unique users are coming to your site. You should ask your provider for the log file. When you receive the log file, you can either get an expert to help you analyze it or you can make estimates. Teaching you to analyze log files is beyond the scope of this book; however, there is one quick method to estimate the number of unique users.

First, determine how many images you have per page on your Web site. If you average 10 images per Web page, and have 10,000 entries in the log file, simply divide the number of entries by the number of images. Your total is 1,000 unique users to your Web site. This is an approximation. If you learn to read log files, you can ascertain which parts of your Web site are heavily trafficked.

The most accurate way to learn the number of hits on your Web site is with a page counter. This device simply increases in number each time the page is viewed by the user. Because each page on the Web site can have its own counter, you can easily see how many times each page has been accessed. Page counters will also display the number of people who have visited that site. Displaying such information builds perceived value. Implementing page counters involves special programming, so ask an expert to assist you in implementing one for your Web site.

In addition to log files and page counters, forms like guest books are great for generating demographic information. How do you get someone to fill out a form? Most obviously, you ask questions in a form, which a user fills out and submits to you via e-mail. You can collate the information to use it any way you like. Many types of demographics can be solicited in this manner. You can ask questions about improving your site: Is it too slow? Does it provide enough graphics? Too many graphics? Is it easy to use? Internet users, in general, like to give their opinions. Once you get demographic information, you can use standard methods of market analysis to understand your audience. A good database system can help collate the information you received from your forms.

Cyberpublicity is both art and science. The basic information in this chapter offers a foundation for cyberpublicity and can guide your Internet and marketing promotions effort. However, the intricacies of planning effective marketing are a much broader topic.

Publicity is an ongoing part of your marketing program, not a one-shot effort you make when you launch your business. With a clear publicity plan, you have goals for how you want your company portrayed in the media over the long term, and some tactics, weapons, and targets to help you achieve those goals—which brings us to the next chapter.

~

Letting People Know About You: Your Marketing Plan

At the beginning of chapter 10, I gave my own interpretation of marketing. Different specialists see this very important function from their individual perspectives. To Roy Sloane, president of Advertising Management, a well-established, home-based ad agency, the definition of marketing is "planning to sell."

In preparing to promote your business, especially on a modest budget, it's imperative that you draw up a careful plan. Besides allocating the dollars and cents you'll be spending, I urge you to calculate the number of hours you'll have available each week to market your product or service. During the first year of a service business, the owner can easily spend two-thirds of her time marketing! In the case of a career counselor, for example, that might include introductory meetings with therapists who can refer patients, and lunchtime speeches to professional groups. Later on, someone else will have to do either the marketing or the actual service providing for you. One of my clients, an architect who now has a staff of nine, reports spending 75 percent of his time on bringing in business. That figure includes soliciting prospects in person, writing proposals, supervising preparation of promotional materials (newsletter, ads, trade show fliers), and extensive telephone contact.

Once you're established, experts advise spending 1 to 10 percent of an annual small-business budget on advertising. As you start out, set aside a reasonable amount of money to spread the word about your business. It's an investment in your success. Then figure out what you can do with this sum. (*Advertising Age* publishes an annual survey of advertising costs, so you can check out industry averages in your field when you want to know what the competition is spending.)

Select from the dozens of inexpensive marketing methods in the previous chapters or use your own approach. As your business and your budget grow, you may want to consider other marketing techniques I omitted because they cost more than a $2,000 start-up company can afford: radio, television, direct mail, outdoor ads, national magazines, card packs, promotional items, major directories, catalogs, a tele-marketing service, etc. When you reach that level, find a small ad agency accustomed to working with companies the size of yours to help you create an effective, professional campaign.

Each time I write six-month or one-year marketing plans for clients, I begin by identifying some important details. On the following pages, I've created sample marketing plans at realistic prices in the current economy for two different (fictitious) service businesses.

PERFECT PROOFREADING Service

1. *Who is your target customer?*
   - Book and magazine publishers; other businesses that produce a large volume of lengthy documents
2. *What are your marketing goals?*
   - To show prospective clients how Perfect Proofreading can help them
   - To position Perfect Proofreading as experienced, reliable, careful, and knowledgeable

- ✦ To build awareness of Perfect Proofreading's existence
- ✦ To generate introductory conversations with prospects

3. *How can your message be conveyed?*
- ✦ By classified ads in trade journals of the publishing field; by direct mail to a self-compiled list of managers at target companies

4. *What are your key selling points?*
- ✦ Training and experience of the owner
- ✦ Consistent attention to detail
- ✦ Prompt service
- ✦ Reasonable fees

5. *How much time can you spend on networking?*
- ✦ _____ hours per week.
- ✦ Here are some places to do it: Breakfast, lunch, or dinner meetings of any local publishers' group. Let them get to know you. Always carry a business card. Sympathize with their complaints about the scarcity of good proofreaders; propose a solution: *you.*

6. *Proposed marketing budget*
- ✦ Classified ad (two lines) in two trade journals each month
  6 months @ $48 per month $288
- ✦ Introductory sales letter to all nearby publishers and appropriate businesses (perhaps 200)
  Copywriting and word processing $250
  Photocopied onto your letterhead $15
  First-class postage for 200 letters $64
  200 envelopes $20
  TOTAL $349
- ✦ Follow-up phone calls to everyone who received a letter. Ask for a brief introductory meeting or find out how often you should check in to see if your services are needed
  200 × 35¢ per call $70
- ✦ Second sales letter (about three months later) to remind them

you're still around and to include a testimonial statement from one of your first—extremely satisfied—clients

TOTAL $349

SIX-MONTH TOTAL $1,056

Note: A good addition to these sales letters is enclosing a Rolodex card, with a tab reading PROOFREADER. In basic black and white, they can be offset-printed for about $100 per thousand. They make it very easy for prospects to keep your name and number handy.

GREENTHUMB, a plant-sitting business

1. *Who is your target customer?*
   + Anyone within a ten-mile radius who needs indoor or outdoor plants taken care of while he or she is out of town on business or vacation. Target customers are likely to be employed, probably in professional or managerial jobs, with household income over $50,000.
2. *What are your marketing goals?*
   + To let potential customers know GREENTHUMB exists
   + To position the service as reliable and affordable
   + To offer prospective clients peace of mind while they're away
3. *How can your message be conveyed?*
   + On inviting fliers placed in mailboxes of residents in all suitable nearby communities
   + In small ads and write-ups in community newspapers
   + At block parties and other town events where a table displaying attractive plants will draw attention
4. *What are your key selling points?*
   + Reliability. Use a quotation from a satisfied "client" (a friend whose plants you tended). Include your bonding number, if appropriate. Cite any community or public service awards won by founder.
   + Training of GREENTHUMB staff. (Courses in horticulture, botany?

Teaching experience at any gardening institution?)

* Love of plants. Feature a photo of owner in her own leafy indoor or outdoor garden.

5. *How much time will you have for networking?*

* _____ hours per week.

* Here are some places to do it: Give talks to local women's groups and church or other religious groups about making plants healthier, the best plants for a garden in our climate or environment, growing things you can eat, etc.

* Offer a demonstration at a health club, YMCA, or any other appropriate group about which plants can provide herbal cures for assorted conditions, or better air for members to breathe, and any other relevant topic.

6. *Proposed marketing budget*

* Flier:

  Copywriting $50
  Desktop publishing design, typesetting, layout .. $50
  Offset printing (one color) 5,000–10,000 .... $100
  Distribution by a service @ $25 per 1,000 .... $150
  TOTAL $350

* Ads in community newspaper every other
  week @ $25 .... $325

* Press release to all local papers announcing opening
  of GREENTHUMB: copywriting and postage $80

* Second press release announcing the first noteworthy
  episode (e.g., a rare plant you've been tending, a celebrity
  whose garden you water, a discovery about local gardens,
  your free tip sheet on how to grow healthier houseplants)
  at GREENTHUMB $80

* Booth at annual community fair, arts and crafts sale;
  any local event your prospects may attend $75

SIX MONTH TOTAL $910

You may want to count your announcements as part of your marketing budget, although I consider them a business expense apart from marketing. A blank marketing form you can use for your planning follows. I invite you to photocopy it so you can make changes easily, or use it later on, for your second six-month plan.

Since you're going to spend a significant sum to spread the word about your business, it's vital to keep track of which method actually works. Always ask, "How did you hear about us?" whenever anyone contacts you. The easiest way to do this is to keep a tally card by the phone and check off each source as first-time calls are received. Over the years, I've evolved a tracking sheet that's set up in categories according to my outreach methods, which include ads, direct mail, directories, trade shows, giving talks, writing articles, and sending a newsletter. I leave one horizontal line for each of those, giving each direct-mail promotion its own line. I also have separate sections for referrals and repeat customers. I keep each tally for one year (in my case, from July 1 to June 30), and at the end of the year I evaluate what is or isn't working. To get a firmer picture of what I'm spending for each sale, I have four vertical columns:

COST (in dollars or hours)	INQUIRIES ONLY	ACTUAL SALES	AVERAGE SALE

This approach has been especially helpful in letting me see which method brings in many inquiries (making it seem highly effective, right?), but virtually no sales. In your first six months, you'll learn a great deal about who responds to which marketing method, so be sure you're keeping score.

Here are two sample entries from this year's tally sheet:

	COST (in dollars or hours)	INQUIRIES ONLY	ACTUAL SALES	AVERAGE SALE
HUMOROUS POSTCARD	$300	2	3	$900
NWU JOB LINE	$ 10	1	1	$575

Six-Month Marketing Plan for:

_____

1. Who is your target customer? Write everything you know about the individual or business likely to want your service (or product):

2. What are your marketing goals during your first year?

3. What is your marketing budget?
   TOTAL .... $ _____

4. How can your message be conveyed?
   MEDIUM #1 _____ .... $ _____
   MEDIUM #2 _____ .... $ _____
   MEDIUM #3 _____ .... $ _____
   TOTAL .... $ _____
   (Total should not exceed your marketing budget in item #3!)

5. What are your key selling points?

6. How much time can you devote to networking?
   _____ hours per week.

7. Where are the opportunities in your area?

The time you spend in networking should begin to pay off, gradually. To maximize the impact, it's up to you to cultivate the network you're building. In the case of Perfect Proofreading, the owner should take each business card she collects at a professional association get-together and carefully mark it with where she met this individual. She should jot down the date and anything specific that they discussed. For example, if an editor was pregnant when they met, it would be nice to ask, "How's the baby?" on a follow-up call. And those follow-up calls are essential. No one is likely to remember someone she met briefly at a meeting six or eight months ago. You have to cultivate those recollections. Keep your name in front of people you think may be able to recommend or even hire you in the future. Make sure to call or send something every three months. (Here's a case where those little newsletters or Rolodex cards can be very useful.) If you make it easy for people to think of you—they will.

Networking is often abused because people forget it is a reciprocal relationship: both parties are supposed to benefit. When you come across an obscure article you think would interest someone with whom you discussed this very topic, send it along with a nice, brief note. If the Perfect Proofreading owner stumbles on just the kind of child-care service for which the pregnant editor was looking, she could call with the information, and impress the editor with her thoughtfulness. Guess who the editor will think of the following week when a co-worker says, "I'm desperate for a proofreader"?

~

Resources: Where to Go for Free or Low-Cost Assistance

*T*he American entrepreneur is very fortunate because a wealth of free or inexpensive resources is available. In the 1990s, one often hears how aspiring capitalists in Eastern Europe struggle to find out how to run a profit-making business. In the United States, expert guidance is as close as your telephone or your computer.

Everyone who ever started a business surmounted the same obstacles you're facing, so do not hesitate to ask others for input. Reinventing the wheel is a waste of your time and energy—both of which you'll need to start your business!

This chapter supplies general information on how to access the major types of assistance. The Appendix provides additional specific details.

Courses and Training Programs

With the growth in entrepreneurship, many colleges and universities have added courses for small-business owners to their adult education offerings. In addition to general courses on starting your own business, you can bolster your know-how in key areas like sales, marketing, accounting, and financial management. Call the local higher education institutions to see if they have a continuing education department, and, if so, request a catalog of courses. These types of classes are usually offered evenings and weekends and are generally very reasonable in price.

Professional associations often give special workshops and seminars, which can be extremely valuable because they focus on specific concerns in your own field. Check with groups in your industry to see if they sponsor (or recommend) any courses in your own geographic area.

I've taken several adult education courses in my field at a major university or professional association. Two classes, in particular, were very useful and well worth the time they required. A one-day course on selling skills helped me solve some of the consistent difficulties I was then encountering. A Saturday workshop on pricing and negotiating at the Graphic Artists Guild turned out to be crucial to my financial success because it made me realize I had been undercharging for all my services. (Many courses are exactly as good as the instructor, so ask around to see if anyone you know has ever taken a course with the particular instructor.)

For a sole proprietor, stimulating classroom discussion with colleagues can offer reinforcement, feedback, and fresh perspectives. An added benefit of taking some classes is the opportunity for networking. The other students will know about the business you're beginning and can tell their acquaintances about your services and products.

American Women's Economic Development Corporation (AWED) gives ongoing courses for new business owners. Headquartered in New York City, it has expanded to other U.S. cities. To find out about its courses, call its toll-free number, 800-222-AWED. A fee is charged for the courses.

Other groups that may sponsor training programs for small-business owners are your local chamber of commerce, and the SBA. Watch the business pages of your newspaper for announcements about these programs. You can contact the nearest SBA office by finding its phone number in the Government Blue Pages of your telephone book. This kind of seminar is usually nominally priced.

Information and Counseling

The SBA offers two wonderful sources for free advice. Its long-running SCORE program has chapters all over the country. At your local SCORE office, an experienced businessperson can answer all your questions, give you specific information about regulations and requirements in your state, and direct you to other sources of assistance. To find the nearest SCORE office, access SCORE information at the SBA's toll-free number, 800-8-ASK-SBA.

The other SBA program, from which I have received excellent counseling, is the Small Business Development Center (SBDC), which operates in most states, usually based at a college. Ask your local SBA office to give you the phone number of an SBDC program. SBDC also provides free, one-to-one counseling. Many local programs also offer workshops and seminars on special topics, such as taxes, computer skills, or business plans. If not free, they are inexpensive.

Another source of counseling, for a fee, is AWED. It offers one-hour individual sessions at its offices, and even provide telephone counseling for people who cannot get to AWED. Both these services require advance appointments. AWED has a hotline service, which, according to its brochure, "enables women entrepreneurs across the country to get answers to urgent questions from experts." Available Monday through Friday during business hours, the hotline charges an hourly rate for up to sixty minutes of phone counseling. For any of these counseling services, call 800-222-AWED.

Some professional associations have a mentor program or a system for directing members to appropriate sources of information. The SBA runs a well-known national mentoring program, for which you have to fill out a formal application, available at your SBA office.

With any kind of advisory service, your satisfaction depends upon the knowledge of the consultant and the rapport between the two of you. Some women entrepreneurs have told me they were unhappy with the assistance they received at one or another of the sources recommended in this section. In my own experience, the consultant I met at my local SBDC was so helpful (and reassuring) that I went back to see him, or called with brief questions, anytime I encountered a problem in his areas of expertise. I still consider him a mentor.

My hint for maximizing the value of your quest for assistance is to be as precise as you can when making an appointment. Tell the receptionist what your main concerns are. Ask for the specialist who is best informed about this particular topic. Before you phone, check with any business owners you know who have ever used the service. Ask if they would recommend you specify a certain consultant.

Professional Associations

You can probably tell by reading this book that I am a strong proponent of joining organizations appropriate to my work. My feeling is, why struggle alone when other people in the same industry share so many of my concerns? As a member of six professional groups, I receive different benefits from each of them, but here are some of the major reasons people join a business association:

- ❧ group rates on various types of insurance
- ❧ recommendations to suppliers of services you may need
- ❧ up-to-date information on laws affecting your business
- ❧ news of recent developments on the technical side of your work
- ❧ a formal or informal job bank offering leads to potential clients
- ❧ workshops or seminars on topics important to members
- ❧ discounts on supplies
- ❧ more experienced peers you can turn to for guidance
- ❧ a chance to exchange ideas with colleagues

Professional groups provide support and a base for business, but new entrepreneurs often hesitate to join because of the time and cost. I'm convinced the advantages outweigh any imagined disadvantages. As you start your business, please consider joining at least one association. Besides providing peerless opportunity for networking, these organizations can bring many other rewards.

Often, trade groups keep track of current rates and salaries and release a yearly compilation for members. It's hard to find out what colleagues or competitors charge, so this information saves you time and keeps you from underpricing. Professional groups often have sample contracts tailored to their members' needs. You can modify and use these contracts in your own business.

Associations can help you keep up-to-date on new techniques in your field with continuing education programs, workshops, or seminars. While these may be open to the public, members pay a lower fee. Professional groups that certify practitioners in their field will guide you to appropriate courses and training.

Many groups publish a newsletter, journal, or directory, providing news of relevant activities and issues, plus information about who's doing what in your field. Members may not make every meeting, so organizations often summarize guest lectures in their publications or make tapes available. If advertising is accepted, you can notify colleagues about what you do.

Informally, too, professional groups are the best way to learn of work opportunities for your business. Through casual conversations at monthly meetings, you can find out about a prospect who could use your service or product.

Two of the groups to which I belong have a job line, for which a slight fee ($10 or $15) is charged in addition to membership. These job lines led me to the contract for my third book and to a column in a national trade magazine, among other rewards. Another of my associations publishes and distributes a directory of all its members. I was recently called by a local business owner who saw my little blurb in the directory, liked what I had to say on the phone, and promptly hired me to write his company's brochure.

On a broader level, professional groups lobby in their members' interests, at state and federal levels. For instance, a coalition of associations, Artists for Tax Equity, defeated a new law that would have burdened thousands of professionals with endless record-keeping.

If you're considering joining an association, but cost is a concern, compare two or more organizations. Attend a few meetings as a guest and explore the advantages of membership. Are you comfortable around these people? Do they meet at a viable time and place for you? Inaccessible meetings will slash your networking opportunities, so weigh the benefits carefully. Remember, dues for a professional organization are tax deductible.

When you decide to join a group, plan to be visible: serve on a committee, write for its publication, give a talk. The benefits correlate directly to involvement. Introduce yourself to everyone whenever you're at a meeting—let people know about you and your work so they'll think of you for assignments, subcontracts, or services that they don't offer.

Utilize your membership to practice or polish a skill you want to develop. By contributing some volunteer labor, you'll help the organization while becoming better known to other members. Try out your public speaking, for example. When I decided newsletters would be a good addition to my company's repertoire, I told the executive board of a two-year-old professional group I'd recently joined that I felt it was ready for a newsletter. The board readily agreed—as long as I'd volunteer to edit it. (Just as I'd anticipated.) By donating a dozen hours every two months to writing the copy for the newsletter, I soon accumulated several sample issues for my portfolio. They gave me the credibility to convince clients that my firm could produce newsletters; today that item is one of my main profit centers.

To locate associations in your area, look for calendar listings in local and regional business publications and in the business pages of your daily newspaper. Other possible sources are the chamber of commerce or the business section of your library. Look in the *Encyclopedia of*

Associations for all the organizations in your industry. You can call or write to its headquarters for information on the chapter nearest you. Another good source for this information is the Internet. Many associations have their own Web sites and most professions are represented by one or more forums on the Internet. Try a subject or keyword search using one of the major search engines. Hyperlinks from the right sites should yield a wealth of helpful information.

In my experience, every membership, while an investment of both time and money, is an important commitment to your own success.

Getting Government Contracts

Home-based businesses can compete successfully for government contracts. Merry Marks, the owner of Dustbusters, recently completed the first year of a state contract and is awaiting renewal for a second. "No questions on the application ask if the business is home based," Marks reports. "You just have to meet the requirements for the job, which are clearly stated in the specifications. Each set of specs varies— in our industry, from two to fifty pages. Agencies tell you what they need; you tell them what you will charge. For a big project, the work can be immense. Some of our bids are in the $50,000 to $100,000 range."

Procurement expert Terry Clark, president of Clark Consultants, notes, "There are not many contracts for start-up or home-based businesses, unless you have a unique product or service. Usually [the government] wants you to be in business for at least a year. After that you can go through the regular procurement process, at the federal, state, or local level. Depending on the type of contract you're looking for, it can take several weeks to two months to fill out an entire Request for Proposal (RFP). Be sure to follow all the guidelines to the letter; otherwise you can be eliminated," Clark cautions.

To win a government contract, a business owner must first identify the government agencies that need her services. How can you pinpoint likely prospects? A procurement specialist at the nearest SBA office can try to match you with agencies and provide contact names. Ask the SBA for the Bidders' Mailing List form, a one-page questionnaire of about twenty items. By submitting it, you'll automatically receive RFPs in your field.

The *Commerce Business Daily* publishes all announcements of planned purchases by each government agency. (Call 312-353-2950 to subscribe.) It takes about an hour each day to go through it, see what's available, and keep your hand on the pulse of government contracts. Personal contacts will give you an inside track, so try to meet with people at prospective agencies. They can tell you about new RFPs before the newspaper announcement appears.

When corporate trainer Barbara Sacker won her first government contract "the RFP asked for a lot of material," reports Sacker, president of Pro-Action, Inc. "We had to provide samples of handouts, a full curriculum, and biographies of each presenter, with everything in triplicate. Some RFPs have short deadlines, so I suggest having all your prototypes and bios ready in advance."

For a new business, Terry Clark recommends trying to "get into a situation where you can be a subcontractor. Contact the prime contractors in your field, and let them know what you do." To help you find prime contractors, the U.S. Small Business Administration puts out the SBA *Subcontracting Directory*, which lists major contractors for a wide range of services.

For a copy of the directory, as well as helpful advice about government contracts, start by calling the SBA hotline (800-8-ASK-SBA) from a touch-tone phone. From a wide menu, select the procurement code. You'll get all the basic information. Ask for the name and phone number of the consumer marketing representative at the nearest SBA Regional Office. Each of the ten SBA offices has information on opportunities in that region and works closely with other government agencies. A rep in your region will provide you with the SBA's own *Subcontracting Directory*, and can lead you to similar directories put out by other federal agencies.

In some fields, being a woman business owner may prove to be a great asset. If your industry has traditionally had very few female owners, you'll be noticed simply because you're unusual. Many corporations and government agencies participate in special purchasing programs (also known as set-asides), which encourage awarding contracts to women- and minority-owned businesses. Discuss the requirements for becoming certified as a woman-owned business with the nearest SBA office.

Publications

As a business owner, you should subscribe to the trade periodicals in your field to keep up-to-date. If you serve a particular industry, it's worthwhile for you to subscribe to its trade publications so you can stay current with the newest developments and concerns. You become more valuable to clients when they see you as someone who is truly knowledgeable about their business.

I also recommend reading the local business publications to stay in tune with the economic pulse of the community where you operate. It's important for you to have a feel for the general business climate in your own home area. I subscribe to one weekly local business newspaper that helps me see, for example, which industries are especially in need of marketing assistance.

There are countless business magazines from which you can choose. At a business library, browse through the last six issues of any publication to which you're considering subscribing. Ask successful women business owners what they read. From various periodicals, at different times, I've gained insight, encouragement, new ideas, reassurance, or innovative approaches to a problem shared by other entrepreneurs.

I've subscribed to *Entrepreneur*, *Success*, and *Working Woman*, in addition to local periodicals. I've also found *Home Office Computing* relevant and useful to any small-business owner. (Caveat lector: I must confess here that I used to write a column for the publication. However, I would read it even if I hadn't contributed; many of my clients also like it.) I subscribed to *Inc.* for several years; it had one section, "Anatomy of a Start-Up," that gave an excellent picture of what to consider in launching a business. After dozens of issues, I found that most of the material was aimed at executives of companies far larger than mine, and one can read only so much each month. I heartily recommend you skim a few issues of any publication, before subscribing, to see if it feels right for you.

Support System

This resource should be listed first, in terms of its value to you. Especially if you're working alone, it's crucial to have other people to whom you can turn sometimes. Line up friends, relatives, and neighbors who are willing to lend an ear, a shoulder, or whatever you're in need of. In an earlier chapter, I described some ways to find or create a support group. As you seek out resources, please don't neglect this one—we all need it!

The most important advice I can give you is this: don't be afraid to ask for assistance. None of us can be the ultimate expert on every aspect of running a business, and certainly at the beginning, we need all the help we can get. Good luck!

~

Appendix

Associations

American Marketing Association
250 South Wacker Drive, Chicago, IL 60606-5819
(312) 648-0536; (800) AMA-1150; *http://www.ama.org*

American Women's Economic Development Corporation
60 East Forty-second Street, New York, NY 10165
(212) 692-9100; (800) 222-AWED

Association of African-American Women Business Owners
c/o Brenda Alford, Brosman Research, P.O. Box 13933, Silver Spring,
    MD 20911-3933

Direct Marketing Association
1120 Avenue of the Americas, New York, NY 10036-6700
(212) 768-7277

Mother's Home Business Network

P.O. Box 423, East Meadow, NY 11554

(516) 997-7394

National Association of Black Women Entrepreneurs

P.O. Box 1375, Detroit, MI 48231

(313) 341-7400; fax (313) 342-3433

National Association for the Cottage Industry

P.O. Box 14850, Chicago, IL 60614

(312) 472-8116

National Association for Female Executives

30 Irving Place, New York, NY 10003

(212) 477-2200; *http://www.nafe.com*

National Association for the Self-Employed

P.O. Box 61207, Dallas, TX 75261-9968

(800) 232-6273; *http://selfemployed.nase.org*

National Association of State Development Agencies

750 First Street NE, Suite 710, Washington, D.C. 20002

(202) 898-1302

National Association of Women Business Owners

1100 Wayne Avenue, Silver Spring, MD 20910-5630

(301) 608-2590; fax (301) 608-2596

(800) 55-NAWBO (for printed literature)

http://www.nawbo.org

National Association of Women in Construction (NAWIC)

327 South Adams Street, Fort Worth, TX 76104-1081

817-877-5551; fax (817) 877-0324; *http://www.nawic.org*

National Business Incubation Association
20 East Circle Drive, Suite 190, Athens, OH 45701
(614) 593-4331; fax (614) 593-1996; *http://www.nbia.org*

National Federation of Independent Businesses
600 Maryland Avenue SW, Suite 700, Washington, D.C. 20004
(202) 554-9000; *http://www.nfib.org*

National Foundation for Women Business Owners
1100 Wayne Avenue, Suite 830, Silver Spring, MD 20910-5630
(301) 495-4975; fax (301) 495-4979; *http://nfwbo.org*

National Small Business United
1155 Fifteenth Street NW, Suite 1100, Washington, D.C. 20005
(202) 293-8830; fax (202) 872-8543; *http://www.nsbu.org*

Women Construction Owners and Executives, USA
1615 New Hampshire Avenue NW, Suite 402, Washington, D.C. 20009
(202) 363-4822

Government Agencies and Services

Customs Service Public Information Division
U.S. Treasury Department, 1301 Constitution Avenue, Washington,
    D.C. 20229
(202) 927-6724; *http://www.ustreas.gov/treasury/bureaus/customs*

Internal Revenue Service (IRS) Hotline
Taxpayer Information and Education Branch, Taxpayer Service
    Division, Internal Revenue Service, Department of the Treasury,
    1111 Constitution Avenue NW, Washington, D.C. 20274
(800) 829-1040; *http://www.irs.ustreas.gov*

Minority Business Development Agency
Department of Commerce, Washington, D.C. 20230
(202) 482-4547; *http://www.doc.gov/agencies/mbda/index.html*

Office of Small Business Research and Development
National Science Foundation, 4201 Wilson Boulevard, Arlington, VA
    22230
(703) 306-1234; *http://www.nsf.gov/sbe/srs/ffrdc*

Office of Small and Disadvantaged Business Utilization
Department of Commerce, Fourteenth Street between Constitution
    and Pennsylvania Avenues, NW, Washington, D.C. 20230
(202) 482-1472

Small Business Administration (SBA) Hotline
(800) 8-ASK-SBA

Small Business Innovation Research Program
Office of Technology, Small Business Administration, 409 Third
    Street SW, Washington, D.C. 20416
(202) 205-6450; *http://www.sba.gov*

Other Organizations Providing Assistance

National Minority Business Council
235 East Forty-second Street, New York, NY 10017
(212) 573-2385; *http://www.nmbc.org*

National Minority Supplier Development Council
15 West Thirty-ninth Street, 9th floor, New York, NY 10018
(212) 944-2430; *http://www.trainingforum.com/ASN/NMSDC/
    index.html*

Small Business Export Hotline
(800) 243-7232

U.S. International Trade Commission
http://www.usitc.gov

Books

Azar, Brian. *The Business Survival Kit for the Nineties: A Handbook for Entrepreneurs and Salespeople.* Rockaway, N.Y.: The Sales Catalyst, 1990.

Berkman, Robert I. *Find It Fast: How to Uncover Expert Information on Any Subject.* New York: Harper & Row, 1987.

Bohigian, Valerie. *How to Make Your Home-Based Business Grow.* New York: New American Library, 1984.

Crawford, Tad. *Legal Guide for the Visual Artist.* 3rd ed. New York: Allworth Press, 1989.

Edwards, Paul and Sarah. *Working from Home.* Los Angeles, Calif.: Jeremy P. Tarcher, Inc., 1990.

Girardi, Joe. *How to Sell Anything to Anybody.* New York: Warner Books, 1977.

Hopkins, Tom. *How to Master the Art of Selling.* New York: Warner Books, 1982.

Hyatt, Carole. *The Woman's Selling Game.* New York: Warner Books, 1979.

Kiam, Victor. *Going for It. How to Succeed As an Entrepreneur.* New York: William Morrow & Co., 1986.

Lesko, Matthew. *Getting Yours.* New York: Penguin Books, 1987.

Lewis, Kathleen. *How to Start and Run a Child Care Agency.* Brooklyn, N.Y.: Pinch Sitters, Inc., 1991.

Mancuso, Joseph. *The Small-Business Resource Guide.* New York: Prentice-Hall/Simon & Schuster, 1989.

Parinello, Al. *On the Air . . . How to Get on Radio and Television Talk Shows . . . And What to Do When You Get There.* Norwood, N.J.: Al Parinello, 1991

∼

Index

Page numbers in italics refer to sample forms and illustrations

Books from Allworth Press

The Money Mirror: How Money Reflects Women's Dreams, Fears, and Desires by Annette Lieberman and Vicki Lindner (softcover, 6 × 9, 232 pages, $14.95)

The Secret Life of Money: How Money Can Be Food for the Soul by Tad Crawford (softcover, 5¹/₂ × 8¹/₂, 304 pages, $14.95)

Old Money: The Mythology of Wealth in America by Nelson W. Aldrich, Jr. (softcover, 6 × 9, 340 pages, $16.95)

The Copyright Guide by Lee Wilson (softcover, 6 × 9, 192 pages, $18.95)

The Trademark Guide by Lee Wilson (softcover, 6 × 9, 192 pages, $18.95)

The Patent Guide by Carl W. Battle (softcover, 6 × 9, 192 pages, $18.95)

Legal-Wise: Self-Help Legal Guide for Everyone, Third Edition by Carl W. Battle (softcover, 8¹/₂ × 11, 208 pages, $18.95)

Your Living Trust and Estate Plan: How to Maximize Your Family's Assets and Protect Your Loved Ones by Harvey J. Platt (softcover, 6 × 9, 256 pages, $14.95)

The Internet Research Guide by Timothy K. Maloy (softcover, 6 × 9, 208 pages, $18.95)

The Internet Publicity Guide by V. A. Shiva (softcover, 6 × 9, 208 pages, $18.95)

How to Start and Succeed as an Artist by Daniel Grant (softcover, 6 × 9, 224 pages, $18.95)

An Actor's Guide—Your First Year in Hollywood by Michael Saint Nicholas (softcover, 6 × 9, 256 pages, $16.95)

Please write to request our free catalog. If you wish to order a book, send your check or money order to Allworth Press, 10 East 23rd Street, Suite 400, New York, NY 10010. Include $5 for shipping and handling for the first book ordered and $1 for each additional book. Ten dollars plus $1 for each additional book if ordering from Canada. New York State residents must add sales tax.

If you wish to see our catalog on the World Wide Web, you can find us at Millennium Production's Art and Technology Web site: *http://www.arts-online.com/allworth/home.html* or at *allworth.com*